Hidden History 5

Another Look at Forgotten Mysteries, Oddities, and Unknown Stories From True History

by Lenny Flank

Red and Black Publishers, Florida

Also by the author:

Hidden History: A Collection of Forgotten Mysteries, Oddities, and Unknown Stories from True History

Hidden History 2: Another Collection of Forgotten Mysteries, Oddities, and Unknown Stories from True History

Hidden History 3: A New Collection of Forgotten Mysteries, Oddities, and Unknown Stories from True History

Hidden History 4: An Additional Collection of Forgotten Mysteries, Oddities, and Unknown Stories From True History

Museum Pieces: The Forgotten History, Science and Mystery Behind Some of the Most Interesting Museum Exhibits and Historical Places in the World

Museum Pieces 2: More Forgotten History, Science and Mystery Behind Some of the Most Interesting Museum Exhibits and Historical Places in the World

Museum Pieces 3: A New Collection of Forgotten History, Science, and Mystery Behind Some of the Most Interesting Museum Exhibits and Historical Places in the World

Contents

How An American Pilot Secretly Helped to Sink the *Bismarck*

In 1940, things were looking bleak for England. France had fallen to the Nazis, the Luftwaffe was bombing London nightly, and the United States public was isolationist and keeping out of the war. But with great secrecy, the US government was already helping the British war effort, and one secret American action would later pay off spectacularly during the pursuit of a dangerous threat to Britain's survival, the German battleship Bismarck.

After the surrender of France in 1940, England remained as the only surviving challenge to Nazi Germany's complete domination of Europe. To defeat Britain, the Nazis adopted a two-pronged strategy, by air and by sea. In the air, the Luftwaffe would wage the Battle of Britain to destroy the RAF, give the Germans air superiority, and allow a cross-channel invasion of the British Isles. On the sea, meanwhile, the German Navy would wage the Battle of the Atlantic to destroy the English merchant fleet, cut off the crucial supply lines between North America and Britain, and choke off the English supply of food and war materials, forcing the island nation into submission.

Most of the attacks on British merchant shipping would be made by the U-boat fleet. But the German Navy also had two other significant weapons—the battleships *Tirpitz* and *Bismarck*. At a speed of 30 knots, they were the fastest battleships in the world at the time, and their 15-inch main guns were a match for any other battleship. But the *Bismarck* and *Tirpitz* were built primarily as commerce raiders—they were intended to patrol the North Atlantic, intercept merchant convoys, and destroy them. When the Nazis turned their attention to England in the summer of 1940, the *Bismarck* had just been commissioned for duty, and the *Tirpitz* was nearing completion.

The British realized that if the *Bismarck* managed to reach the open Atlantic, her superior speed would make it extremely difficult to find and track her, and she would pose a serious threat to any supply convoys trying to cross the Atlantic. As a result, the British Navy made plans to intercept the *Bismarck* as soon as it left port, in an attempt to stop her from reaching the open sea.

At first, it was a waiting game. The Germans planned to form a single naval task force with both the *Bismarck* and *Tirpitz* and the cruisers *Prinz Eugen* and *Gneisenau.* But construction problems delayed the *Tirpitz,* and the *Gneisenau* was damaged in a bombing raid. For almost a year, the *Bismarck* sat in port.

It was finally decided to wait no longer, and on May 19, 1941, *Bismarck,* accompanied by the cruiser *Prinz Eugen,* left the German port at Gotenhafen and made her way past Denmark towards the Atlantic. She was almost immediately spotted by a Swedish warship who reported the contact to London (the British were already keeping track of her). The Royal Navy dispatched a force, which included the battle-cruiser *Hood* and the new battleship *Prince of Wales,* to intercept the German ships.

When the two forces met on May 24, the result was catastrophic for the British. A single 15-inch shell from the *Bismarck* penetrated through the armored deck of the *Hood* and exploded inside the ship, setting off the *Hood's* ammunition stores and completely destroying it. *Hood* disappeared in an enormous fireball. Of the 1400 crew members, only 3 survived.

Over the next two days, the British ships engaged in brief firefights with the *Bismarck,* and managed to cause some damage. The German commander, Admiral Gunther Lutjens, evaded the British fleet in a series of nighttime maneuvers, and once free, decided to split up his two ships. The *Prinz Eugen* would continue to the Atlantic, while the *Bismarck* would turn and make a run to a port in Nazi-occupied France for repairs. The British Navy, realizing that this was their best opportunity to destroy the battleship, dispatched more ships from its own fleet to the area, and began a series of frantic air searches to try to locate the *Bismarck* before she could reach safety in port.

It was here that the Americans entered the scene.

In 1940, US President Franklin Roosevelt knew that eventually he would have to fight the Nazis, and, despite the public's sentiment against becoming involved in the European war, began taking steps to skirt the very edge of neutrality and give aid to the British. Under the "Lend-Lease" program, the US began to loan aircraft and ships to the British, with the expectation that they would be "returned" later. As part of Lend-Lease, the Americans gave the RAF 200 long-range Catalina PBY amphibious patrol planes, known as "flying boats", to be used for coastal patrol and anti-submarine duty. But, in a secret part of this deal that was entirely illegal under American law, Roosevelt ordered the US Navy to send seventeen active-duty pilots to England along with the Catalinas. With the excuse that they were there to "train" the British pilots, the US Navy fliers were "loaned" to the RAF's Coastal Command 209th Squadron based in Northern Ireland, and immediately began flying combat missions. Usually, each PBY was flown by a British pilot with an American co-pilot.

When the Royal Navy lost contact with the *Bismarck* on May 26, 1941, the PBYs were hastily pressed into service to fly long-range patrols to find the Germans. Already loaded with depth charges for a routine anti-submarine patrol, one of these flying boats, commanded by RAF pilot Dennis Briggs and US Navy co-pilot Leonard "Tuck" Smith, was diverted to the search. They took off from Loch Erne at about 4 in the morning, and set out for the *Bismarck's* last known position.

The weather was awful. A thick cloud layer descended to just a few thousand feet. After six hours of patrolling, Briggs and Smith saw nothing but clouds and empty ocean.

Then, at 10:10am, they caught a lucky break. Through a gap in the clouds, Smith spotted a large ship in the distance. "I sighted what was first believed to be *Bismarck*," he later reported, "bearing 345 at 8 miles. Definite recognition was impossible at the time due to visibility. I immediately took control from 'George' (automatic pilot); started slow climbing turn to starboard, keeping ship sited to Port, while the British officer went aft to prepare contact report. My plan was to take cover in the clouds, get close to the ship as possible; making definite recognition and then shadow the ship from best point of vantage."

But in the clouds, Smith got too close, and when he broke into clear air at 2,000 feet, he was directly over the *Bismarck*. Smith barely had time to think to himself "My God, what have I done?" when the battleship's anti-aircraft guns opened up on him. "The A.A. fire lasted until we were out of range and into the clouds. It was very intense and were it not for evasive action we would have been shot down. The barrage was so close that it shook the aircraft considerably (one man was knocked from his bunk) and the noise of the burst could be heard above the propeller and engine noise. Numerous bursts were observed at close quarters and small fragments of shrapnel could be heard hitting the plane."

While Smith jettisoned his depth charges and took evasive action, Briggs radioed the news to the Royal Navy. "'One battleship." he reported, "bearing 240° five miles, course 150°, my position 49° 33′ north, 21° 47′

west. Time of origin, 1030/26." The *Bismarck* had been found. Smith shadowed the German battleship until he lost it again in the clouds and, with his fuel running low, turned back for home. By the time the PBY landed back at England, the Royal Navy had already dispatched 19 warships to converge on the *Bismarck's* location.

Meanwhile, two unarmed Swordfish torpedo bombers from the nearby British carrier *Ark Royal* had arrived, and were now shadowing the *Bismarck* and giving updated position reports. Admiral Lutjens frantically radioed to the German Navy: "Enemy aircraft maintains contact: wheeled aircraft!" Everyone knew that a "wheeled aircraft" could only have come from an enemy carrier, meaning that British ships were nearby. The Swordfish were soon joined by two more PBYs flying in shifts, both of them with American co-pilots.

But the British were almost too late. The Royal Navy battleships would not reach the *Bismarck* until after dark, when the Germans would likely be able to evade contact, slip through the British net, and escape to safety in a French port. In desperation, the British used the only weapon they had available, the obsolete canvas-covered biplane Swordfish torpedo bombers from the *Ark Royal,* in a desperate attempt to cause enough damage to the *Bismarck* to slow her down and allow the Royal Navy to catch up.

At about 3 in the afternoon, 15 Swordfish reached the battle area. But instead of attacking the *Bismarck,* they mistakenly targeted the British cruiser *Sheffield,* which, due to a miscommunication, was in an area where the British pilots had been told there were no Royal Navy ships. Fortunately, all of the mistakenly-launched torpedoes missed the cruiser, and the Swordfish returned to the *Ark Royal,* were refueled and re-armed, and launched again at the *Bismarck.* It was 7:15pm and would be dark in just a few hours. They would not get another chance.

The "stringbags" droned in on the *Bismarck* at low altitude, skimming just above the waves. Although several Swordfish were hit by anti-aircraft fire, none of them were shot down, and all of them managed to release their torpedoes. Nearly all missed. One struck the *Bismarck* amidships, causing some slight damage to her heavy armor plating. But another torpedo struck the battleship at the stern end, near the propellers, and the shock wave from this explosion jammed the *Bismarck's* rudders. It was an incredibly lucky shot. With her rudders jammed, the *Bismarck* could not steer, and was now plowing along helplessly in a giant circle. She was soon shadowed by a number of British cruisers who, after a brief exchange of fire, carefully kept their distance. As the German crew tried frantically to repair the rudders and restore steering, the British Navy's battleship fleet approached, arriving at around four in the morning.

The *Bismarck* was doomed. Torpedo-firing destroyers harassed her all night, and at first light, the main British fleet moved in and opened fire. Around 11 am on May 27, after several hours of pounding, the German battleship rolled over and sank.

Shortly later, Ensign Leonard Smith was awarded the Distinguished Flying Cross for his actions in locating the *Bismarck.* But because his very presence at the scene was illegal and his mission was a closely-kept secret, it was decades before it could be openly acknowledged.

Titusville PA: The First Oil Well

Today, the oil industry is one of the largest and richest in the world. Vast fortunes are made by oil, countries are governed by it, ecosystems are destroyed by it. And it all began in a little town in northwestern Pennsylvania.

In the first half of the 19th century, the United States, along with most of Europe, was undergoing an economic revolution. The agricultural economy that had dominated life for 10,000 years was being replaced by a new manufacturing economy. The "Industrial Revolution" produced wealth on a scale that had never been seen before, and created an entire "middle class" of shopkeepers and managers who had something most people had never had before—a disposable income. And with their new income, the rising middle classes were able to afford luxuries that only the aristocracy had been able to obtain previously.

One of these new luxuries was the lighted house. For centuries, the feudal peasantry had lived, literally, in the dark. The only widely-available source of indoors light were candles, and these were expensive and didn't work very well. The Industrial Revolution, though, introduced something new—the mass-produced glass oil lamp. These were able to light a room far better (and more safely) than candles. The only available source of oil, however, was whale oil, extracted at sea by a (mostly American) fleet that spent years on a single voyage and, as often as not, returned empty-handed—and the whales were already being over-hunted to such an extent that entire species were being threatened with extinction. The demand for whale oil was far outgrowing the ability to supply it.

Chemists had already found a better fuel. For centuries, petroleum tar and raw crude oil had been seeping to the surface at various places from underground pools. These materials had been used by local people for waterproofing and lubrication, and in the early 1800's were also being bottled and sold as quack medicines. But, when chemically distilled, crude petroleum from the ground produced "kerosene", a liquid lamp fuel which burned more brightly than whale oil, and with less soot and odor. By the 1850's there were already a number of commercial ventures that collected crude oil in places where it seeped to the surface and sold it as lubricating oil and as distilled kerosene.

In 1854, two lawyers from New Hampshire named George Bissell and Jonathan Eveleth formed a corporation called the Pennsylvania Rock Oil Company, in the little farming village of Titusville PA. At "Oil Creek" just outside of town, there was a natural seep where crude petroleum could be gathered in small amounts as it collected at the surface. For the next several years, they made a living by gathering 2 or 3 barrels of oil per month.

It was, however, apparent to all that this would not be enough; the only way to obtain crude oil in sufficient amounts would be to drill underground to it, rather than waiting for it to seep naturally to the surface. But at the time the only drilling technology that existed was for digging water wells, and the method used to drill through soil to the water table did not work when drilling through solid rock for oil. Every company that attempted to drill down to the oil deposits, including Bissell's, failed to reach the required depth.

Then, in 1857, Bissell met a former railroad conductor named Edwin Drake, who happened to be staying in the same hotel in Titusville. Drake owned a few shares of stock in the Rock Oil Company and had traveled to Pennsylvania from New York to visit the petroleum seeps. Bissell and Eveleth had been looking to hire someone who could travel back and forth to inspect their oil fields, which were scattered around western Pennsylvania, and Drake, who as a former railroad employee could ride the trains for free, fit the bill. More importantly, Drake also had some experience with drilling water wells. The three men formed a partnership to find a workable method of drilling for oil, and called it the Seneca Oil Company. Drake was hired as company president.

Their first well, in October 1858, was a disaster: the drill reached a depth of just 16 feet, and a worker who was using an open flame to examine it touched off an oil fire that destroyed the wooden derrick.

It was then that Drake had an idea—instead of trying to drill directly through the rock to reach the oil, he would push a hollow iron tube, called a "drive pipe", down ahead of the drill to break up the rock layer and make it easier for the drill to penetrate, and also prevent collapses. He hired a local blacksmith to make the drive pipe and drill, and to run the operation. The crude drilling apparatus managed to go down about three feet a day. When the Seneca Oil Company ran out of cash during the drilling, Drake borrowed money on his own and continued work.

On Saturday, August 27, 1859, at a depth of 69 feet, the drill bit struck an oil pocket. By the next morning, a large pool of oil had oozed to the surface. Drake's well produced about 20 barrels a day, more than a whaling ship could bring back in an entire year. For the next 40 years, Pennsylvania would supply over half of the world's petroleum—until even larger oilfields were discovered in Texas. The Oil Age had begun.

But the man who started it, died in poverty. Edwin Drake had never patented his "drive pipe" idea, and never received a dime from all the new oil companies that were getting rich using his invention. After the original Titusville well caught fire and burned down, Drake drilled two more wells before leaving the oil business, worked briefly as a Justice of the Peace, and died in Bethlehem PA in 1880.

Bunker Hill: The Most Famous Battle Lost by the US

It may be the most famous battle of the Revolutionary War. But the Battle of Bunker Hill did not happen the way most Americans today think it did. It didn't even happen on Bunker Hill. And it was the British who won the fight.

When the American Revolution began with the battles at Lexington and Concord, the bulk of the British Army was garrisoned in the city of Boston. The English government, hoping to quell the rebellion quickly, dispatched three Generals, Clinton, Burgoyne and Howe, along with additional troops, from London to reinforce General Gage in Boston. They arrived in early June 1775.

While Boston was surrounded by towns filled with rebellious militia, the city itself was controlled by the British Navy. The only potential danger lay in the possibility that the colonial rebels might get cannons into position on some of the hills surrounding Boston, allowing them to shell the British ships in the harbor. To prevent that from happening, the British made plans to send troops to occupy the hills.

Through sympathetic civilians, the colonial militia commanders heard about the plan. To counter it, the rebel commander General Israel Putnam ordered Colonel William Prescott to take a force of about 1,000 Massachusetts and Connecticut militiamen and fortify Bunker Hill, which overlooked the harbor. Somehow, though, the colonial force ended up instead on Breed's Hill, about 600 yards away—perhaps because Prescott thought it would be easier to defend, perhaps because they simply went to the wrong hill. In any case, the colonials spent the night of June 16 digging trenches and building stone and log breastworks on the crest of Breed's Hill. At daybreak, the British ship HMS *Lively* saw the fortifications and opened fire on them; within an hour most of the other warships in the harbor had joined in the bombardment. But by this time the Americans had already finished their trenches, and the cannonade had little effect.

It fell to the British General Howe to remove the rebels. He went ashore with 2,500 troops at about 3pm on June 17. The Americans had about 1,000 militiamen on Breed's Hill; there were several hundred more on nearby Bunker Hill, but most of them refused to advance after the British landing.

Howe probably thought his task would be easy. The American militia were an undisciplined rabble, and his English regulars were the best army in the world—and they outnumbered the militiamen almost three to one. With a direct assault up the hill, Howe concluded, the colonials would break and run away, and the rebellion would be over. With supreme overconfidence, he formed his troops into an extended line, and ordered them to charge.

At the top of the hill, the Americans waited and watched as the red-coated British slowly came up the hill. According to legend, Colonel Prescott had issued the order "Don't shoot until you can see the whites of their eyes." The British troops were only 50 yards away when the colonials opened fire. The effect was devastating: huge holes were ripped in the British ranks, and the entire line faltered, then staggered back down the hill. Dead redcoats lay everywhere. Howe hastily reorganized his troops, formed them into another line—and sent them back up the hill. Again the colonials opened fire at short range, and again the British dropped by the dozens and retreated. Howe was shocked; he had not expected an actual fight with the rebels.

He now ordered his artillery into action, and for some time, British cannon raked the Americans with canisters of grapeshot. And then, for the third time, the British troops were sent up Breed's Hill. By this time, however, the colonial militiamen were running out of powder and ammunition. The redcoats made it to the top of the hill with bayonets fixed, and after a few minutes of brutal hand-to-hand fighting, the Americans, outnumbered and out of ammo, broke and ran. The British, who had lost almost half of their troops killed or wounded, did not pursue them. The entire battle had lasted about two hours.

It was, technically, a British victory; the redcoats had driven their enemy off the battlefield and they stood in possession of the high ground. But it had been purchased at an unacceptably high cost, and the Americans had demonstrated an unexpected willingness to not only stand and fight, but to do so effectively. There would be no quick win here; the American insurgency would become a long bloody quagmire for the British.

Less than a year later, the American General Washington, using British cannon that he had captured from Fort Ticonderoga, once again occupied a series of hills around Boston. The British General Howe, surrounded by hostile civilians and cannons, abandoned the city, and withdrew his command post all the way to Canada.

Was Billy the Kid Granted a Pardon?

Billy the Kid is one of the most famous outlaws of the Old West. But his story has mostly been exaggerated. For at least part of the time he was actually a deputized lawman. And he may have been granted a pardon by the Governor of New Mexico in exchange for cooperating with law enforcement.

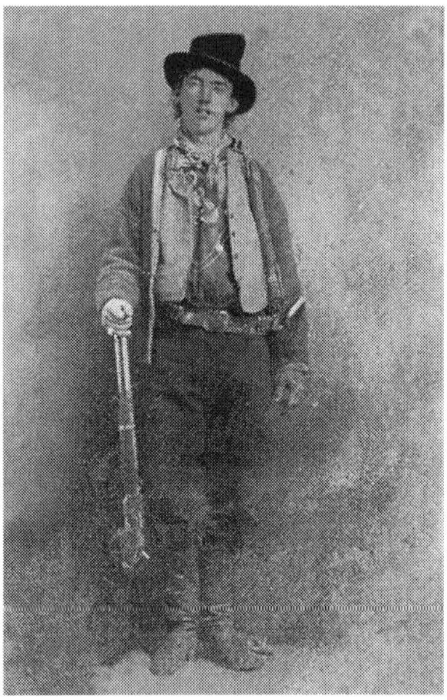

Not much is known about the early life of Billy the Kid. He always told people that he had been born in New York City, and this is confirmed by a birth record of "William Henry McCarty" on September 17, 1859. His mother's name was Catherine, an immigrant who arrived in the US from Ireland with her husband Patrick McCarty. In 1864, Patrick McCarty died, and Catherine shortly later moved in with (and later married) a man named William Antrim. To avoid confusion with the two "Williams", the young boy William began to be referred to by his middle name, "Henry".

In 1870, Catherine, Antrim, young Henry and his younger half-brother Joseph moved to Kansas. When Catherine was diagnosed with tuberculosis, the family moved to Colorado and then to Silver City, New Mexico, where they hoped the hot dry weather would help her health. But in 1874, Catherine died, and William Antrim placed the two boys in foster care and departed for Arizona.

Left to fend for himself, young Henry McCarty fell in with a local desperado called Sombrero Jack, and made a living by petty theft. When Henry was caught with a bundle of stolen laundry, he was arrested, but escaped by climbing up the jail's chimney, and ran to one of his former foster families, who gave him some money and put him on a stagecoach to Arizona. There, Henry, about 16 years old, was taken in by another outlaw, a thief named John Mackie. They made a living by stealing horses from the nearby US Army outpost.

In August 1877, Henry McCarty, now using the name "Henry Antrim" and already known, from his short stature and slight build, as "The Kid", got into a bar fight with a local blacksmith named Windy Cahill, managed to pull out his pistol, and shot him. Now facing murder charges, the teen fled to New Mexico. There, he was taken in by a group of ruffians who called themselves "The Boys", and moved along with them to Lincoln County.

At this time, Lincoln County was run, in the absence of any effective government or law enforcement, by a man named James Dolan, an Irishman who owned the only store in the county (and controlled most of the other businesses as well), hired and fired sheriffs as if they were employees, and, on the side, did some work as a cattle rustler and horse thief. At about the same time as young Henry Antrim and "The Boys" arrived (to work for Dolan and his syndicate), a British immigrant named John Tunstall arrived in town, with a sum of money he had brought from England. Tunstall's intention was to open his own businesses and eventually take over the de facto county government from Dolan. It was the beginning of what became known as "The Lincoln County War".

Although "The Boys" were working for Dolan, Henry Antrim had a falling out with them, and left to join Tunstall as a ranch hand. It was at this time that Henry Antrim began using the name "William H Bonney".

Given that both camps were surrounding themselves with hired gunslingers, an armed conflict was inevitable. It came on February 18, 1878, when an armed posse, deputized by Dolan's appointed Sheriff William Brady, met with Tunstall on the road and, without warning, shot him off his horse. The next day, the local Constable, Richard Brewer, deputized Bonney and other members of the Tunstall gang, and issued an arrest warrant for the Dolan gang members who had killed Tunstall. For the next two years, the Lincoln County War was now an actual war, with two gangs of armed thugs each acting in the name of the law. After Tunstall's death, his supporters became known as "The Regulators", and William Bonney took over leadership and became widely known as "Billy the Kid". In a long series of raids, gunfights and ambushes, 22 men on both sides were killed, including Sheriff Brady.

In 1879, the two gangs reached an uneasy truce. But now a new Territorial Governor, former Union Army General Lew Wallace, moved in to attempt to end the bloodshed. The Governor offered an amnesty to everyone on both sides, as long as they were not currently under indictment. Billy the Kid was under a number of indictments (one for the murder of Sheriff Brady), but he sent a message to the Governor's office that he would testify on behalf of the state if he were also granted amnesty. In March 1879 the two met in Santa Fe to work out the deal. The Governor agreed to a full pardon in exchange for the Kid's testimony. As part of the deal, Bonney agreed to be held in the local jail until after his testimony, when he would be released.

Things didn't turn out that way. After Bonney testified to a grand jury, the local District Attorney, contrary to the Governor's agreement, refused to release him and planned to prosecute him for several murders. Thinking he had been double-crossed by the Governor, Billy the Kid escaped from the jail and fled to the Mexican border region. The Governor placed a $500 bounty on his head. After another shootout in which a Deputy Sheriff was killed, Billy and most of his gang were captured in December 1880 by Sheriff Pat Garrett, who had known Billy the Kid earlier. The Kid was taken to Sante Fe and convicted at trial of murdering Lincoln County Sheriff Brady. He was sentenced to be hanged on May 13, and was transported to Lincoln County for his execution.

In the afternoon of April 28, 1881, Billy the Kid was being held in the upper floor of the courthouse by Deputy Sheriff James Bell and Deputy Sheriff Robert Olinger, who had been amusing himself by taunting the Kid. Shortly after Deputy Olinger left to have lunch in the saloon across the street, Billy the Kid asked Deputy Bell to take him to the outhouse. As they climbed the stairs to return to the jail cell, the Kid shot Bell, who died instantly. According to legend, a sympathizer had stashed a gun for him inside the outhouse; according to the story that Billy the Kid himself told others, he had managed to get one of his hands out of his cuffs, pulled one of Bell's own pistols, and shot him with it.

Across the street, Deputy Olinger heard the shot and ran outside. Billy was in the second floor window, holding Olinger's own shotgun, which had been left behind. "Hello, Bob", he said, and pulled both barrels. Olinger fell dead. Billy the Kid mounted a nearby horse and rode off. He was now the most-wanted man in New Mexico.

It took two months for Sheriff Pat Garrett to track Billy's whereabouts. On the night of July 14, 1881, Garrett went to the home of one of Billy's Mexican girlfriends. What happened next is unclear. According to Garrett's account, he was already there, talking to an acquaintance named Peter Maxwell to find out where Billy was, when the Kid himself unexpectedly walked through the door. Seeing someone in the dark room, Billy asked in Spanish "Who is it?" and pulled a pistol and a knife, whereupon

Garrett drew his own gun and shot him in the chest. In another version put forth by some historians, Garrett already knew the Kid would be there that night and was waiting in ambush, and when Billy entered the room on his way to the kitchen, Garrett shot him without warning.

In the popular legend, Billy the Kid was credited with killing 21 men, "one for each year of his life". In reality, most of those were gang shootouts in which he probably did not fire the fatal shots, but was charged with the murder anyway as part of the gang. Most historians conclude that Billy the Kid himself probably killed only four people—two of those in saloon fights, and two of them being the deputies shot during his escape.

There is only one authenticated photo of Billy the Kid, showing him with a rifle and pistol (though a second photo, believed to depict The Kid along with other members of The Regulators, surfaced in 2015). Based on the photo, in which the revolver holster is at his left hip, it was long believed that the Kid was left-handed. It wasn't until the 1980's that somebody noticed that the loading port on the lever-action rifle in the photo was depicted on the wrong side, and that it was a tintype photo, which produces a mirror image. Properly reversed, the photo would show the pistol on the right hip, making Billy the Kid right-handed after all.

The story of Billy the Kid took a modern turn in 2010, when New Mexico Governor Bill Richardson, a fan of Western history, announced that he was investigating the possibility of fulfilling the offer of amnesty that Territorial Governor Wallace had agreed to in 1879, and might issue a posthumous pardon to Billy the Kid. On his last day in office, however, Richardson announced that although it seemed certain that Wallace had agreed to issue an amnesty, the Kid's actions afterwards, including killing two Deputy Sheriffs in his escape, precluded the possibility of a posthumous pardon.

The Lost State of Franklin

The "lost state" of Franklin is today virtually forgotten. But it almost became what would now be our 51st state, and for a short time it was an independent nation.

In 1783, the newly-independent US was still under the Articles of Confederation. Congress was deeply in debt to France and Spain for the help it had received during the Revolutionary War, but under the Articles, the federal government did not have the authority to levee taxes, and so had no way to pay its foreign debt.

The state of North Carolina, meanwhile, was having troubles of its own. The state had signed a treaty with the local Native American nations (the Cherokee, Chickasaw and Chikamauga), but now there was disagreement over what the treaty actually provided. According to North Carolina, the state's borders extended all the way to the Mississippi River; according to the Natives, they had only agreed to allow the settlers who were already there at the time of the treaty to stay, but the tribes still retained ownership of the land. There were already over 5,000 whites living in western North Carolina, including the large village at Fort Nashborough on the Cumberland River (which would later be renamed Nashville) and White's Fort (later renamed Knoxville). As more settlers moved into the disputed area, a conflict seemed inevitable.

In May 1784, the North Carolina State Legislature decided that it had neither the means nor the money to send militia units all the way to Fort Nashborough to protect the settlers from the increasing number of Cherokee and Chickamauga raids, so they decided to give up their claim to the entire area, and passed an act ceding ownership of the whole of western North Carolina to the US Congress, on the assumption that Congress would sell off the land and use the money to pay its debts. Defending the area against Native attacks (and resolving the legal question of who actually owned the land that the settlers were living on), conveniently enough, would no longer be North Carolina's problem.

Just a few weeks later, however, things were completely reversed by the state elections. Most of the newly-elected legislators were land speculators who themselves owned tracts of land in the disputed area—not only were they afraid that Congress would decide that the Natives had legal title to their land, but they were alarmed by the possibility that even if Congress decided that the Natives had deeded away the land by treaty, the federal government might decide to give the land to Spain or France in lieu of its war debts, thus putting a foreign-controlled area on the state's borders. In a quick vote, the new legislature withdrew its earlier offer and now re-claimed ownership over western North Carolina.

The see-saw of events, quite naturally, led the inhabitants of the disputed area to conclude that North Carolina simply did not want them and would not expend any effort or expense to defend them. So they took matters into their own hands—in August 1784, the three counties in western North Carolina announced that they were seceding from the state and would be forming a new state of their own, to be called "Frankland". In response, North Carolina sent a militia force under the Revolutionary War hero John Sevier, who had won the Battle of King's Mountain, to subdue the rebellious counties. Instead, upon arrival, Sevier, who himself owned a large number of tracts in the disputed area, joined the secessionists. "Frankland" organized an assembly to write a new state constitution, which guaranteed freedom of religion, banned doctors, lawyers and clergy from serving in the legislature, and gave voting rights to all male citizens without property qualifications. This constitution was rejected by the public, however, and was replaced with a new one that was mostly a copy of the state constitution of North Carolina. The new "state's" capitol was established in Jonesborough, Sevier was elected Governor, and in May 1785 a delegation was sent to Congress to petition for Frankland's admission to the Union as the 14th State.

Under the Articles, it took a two-thirds vote of state legislatures to admit a new state. In an attempt to curry favor, Governor Sevier changed the name of the new state from "Frankland" to "Franklin" and asked statesman Benjamin Franklin for help. Franklin politely replied that since he had been in Europe all this time, he didn't know enough about the situation to be of any service. In the end, the new state of "Franklin" received seven votes for admission, but six states, under pressure from North Carolina, noted "no".

The failure of the statehood effort put "Franklin" into an uncomfortable position, and forced Sevier's state government to do the only thing it *could* do—it declared its independence as the Free Republic of Franklin. By the end of 1786, the Republic claimed territory that would later become eight counties, wrote a national constitution, and elected Sevier as President. The "national legislature" appointed a committee to design a flag for the new country (which never completed the task), and plans were made for minting new coinage (in the meantime, American, Spanish and French money was all accepted as legal tender, as well as deerskins, corn, and rum). The State of North Carolina, meanwhile, had established its own parallel government in the territory, including its own courts and tax offices, also based in

Jonesborough, and continued to claim sovereignty over the entire area. In response, the "Republic of Franklin" moved its capitol to Greeneville.

The new Republic, however, was virtually broke and had nothing in the way of resources. In desperation, President Sevier now made a fatal move—he began talks with both the Spanish and the French, each of whom had large colonies nearby, with an eye towards gaining military protection and economic aid. This was something that North Carolina could not tolerate, and an arrest warrant was issued charging Sevier with treason. A militia force was dispatched, commanded by local Colonel John Tipton, with orders to arrest Sevier, disband the "Republic", and return the area to North Carolina's control. In February 1788, when one of Tipton's officers seized a farm owned by Sevier and confiscated it, Sevier responded by sending his own militia troops to Tipton's farm at Johnson City. Two people died in the resulting clash, which became known, melodramatically, as "The Battle of Franklin".

Within Franklin itself, moreover, dissent and division had now appeared. A sizable part of the population wanted to dissolve the Republic and rejoin North Carolina, as a means of gaining protection against the increasing raids from the Cherokee, Chickasaw and Chikamauga tribes (who were, as they saw it, defending their territory from invaders). In August 1788, Sevier was briefly arrested by North Carolina militia, and was promptly freed by a group of local citizens. But by February 1789 it was all over. Sevier's "Republic" had completely collapsed and lost all public support. Sevier surrendered and, after swearing an oath of allegiance to North Carolina, was given a command in the state militia and fought against the Native tribes. A small group of secessionist holdouts, calling themselves "The Republic of Lesser Franklin", finally gave up in 1791.

After Sevier's surrender, the State of North Carolina once again turned over its western counties to Congress, to be organized as part of the "Southwest Territory". Sevier was elected as Territorial Governor, and in 1796, when the area that had formerly been the "State of Franklin" was admitted to the Union as the State of Tennessee, Sevier became the new state's first Governor. Col Tipton was elected to the Tennessee State Legislature.

And the "State of Franklin" faded into historical obscurity. Its most enduring legacy is a provision that was written into the new Constitution in 1789, specifically to prevent future headaches of the sort caused by "Frankland's" secession from North Carolina: "Article IV Section 3: New States may be admitted by the Congress into this Union; but no new States shall be formed or erected within the Jurisdiction of any other State; nor any State be formed by the Junction of two or more States, or parts of States, without the Consent of the Legislatures of the States concerned as well as of the Congress."

Black Beetle: The First Jet-Engine Locomotive

Today, we take ultra-highspeed "bullet trains" for granted. But back in the 1960s they were still just a concept, and no one was sure how a super-fast train would work. One of the oddest experiments of the time was the Black Beetle, the world's first jet-engine locomotive.

In the early 1960s, passenger rail was in big trouble. The US was in the final stages of completing the largest cross-country highway system in the world, the automobile had replaced the train as the transport of choice, and the remaining passenger rail lines were in serious decline.

Two of the remaining train lines were the Pennsylvania Railroad and the New York Central Railroad, who were competing for the shrinking commuter market in the northeast. In 1965, the New York Central believed it could gain an advertising advantage over its rival (and draw more commuter passengers back to the railroads) if it could field a super-fast train, and turned to its Department of Technical Research, based in Cleveland, to help. The department's Assistant Director, Don Wetzel, had formerly been an Air Force pilot, and he came up with a bold idea for an ultra-highspeed passenger train—a jet-powered locomotive. After talking it over with the company president, Alfred Perlman, Wetzel was given an ordinary Budd RDC-3 "Beeliner" locomotive, number M-497, and was given the green light to perform some experiments. It would be a great publicity stunt, and who knows, it just might lead to a viable commercial project.

At a scrapyard in Tucson, Wetzel was able to buy two surplus General Electric J-47 turbojet engines, for $2500 each. In the 1950's the US Air Force had used the J-47 engine to power a variety of frontline combat aircraft, from the F-86 fighter to the B-47 Stratojet nuclear bomber. But production of the J-47 had ceased in 1956 and it was now obsolete. The engines were particularly convenient for Wetzel because, although they had been run on jet fuel, they could also be easily adapted to run on diesel.

Wetzel purchased a surplus engine pod from an old B-36 Peacemaker nuclear bomber. The intercontinental bomber had supplemented its piston-engines with two jet pods, each containing two Model 19 variants of the J-47 with 5200 pounds of thrust each. Wetzel extracted the engines and altered them to use diesel fuel, then mounted them on top of the Beeliner. The locomotive was modified with a specially-built fairing at the front to make it more streamlined, and most of the interior was emptied and then packed with test instruments. Finally, the engine was given a glossy red and black paint job, which led to it being christened "The Black Beetle".

In the summer of 1966 the Beetle was ready for testing. Wetzel volunteered himself as the "test pilot", and selected a 68-mile portion of track that ran from Stryker OH to Butler IN. It was the longest straight stretch of railroad that the New York Central had. Because this line was used only for freight, it did not meet the standards for passenger track, and the rails had to be replaced and upgraded.

The first test was on July 23, 1966, followed by another test on July 24. The highest speed that was officially recorded was 183.681mph—but at the moment this measurement was made the train was decelerating, so it likely hit at least 190mph. It remains the fastest speed recorded for a light-rail passenger train in the US.

Despite her record-setting run, however, the Black Beetle had an ignominious end. Jet-powered locomotives were simply not practical, and the concept was dropped. The Beetle's J-47 engines were removed and used in another experimental project—jet-powered snow-blowers that were carried on a special car to remove ice and snow from the tracks. The Beetle's locomotive was restored to diesel power and sent to New York City with the Penn Central Line (Penn Central was a merger between the New York Central and the Pennsylvania Railroad). When Penn Central was purchased by Conrail in 1976, the obsolete Beeliner was sold to the New York MTA, which used it for spare parts and then scrapped it in 1984.

Mata Hari: The Real Story

The name "Mata Hari" has become virtually synonymous with "espionage". But despite her fame, it is not at all clear that the World War One exotic dancer was ever actually a spy for anyone.

As an exotic dancer and performer (and a courtesan to much of Europe's wealthy elite), Mata Hari gave out so many embellished tales of her life that today it is virtually impossible to sort them all out. It is known that her real name was Margaretha Geertruida Zelle, and she was born in 1876 in Holland as the daughter of an oil investor. When Zelle was just 13, her father lost his fortune, and two years later her mother died. She was separated from her three younger brothers and was sent to live with her godfather. While attending a private school that trained girls to become teachers, the 16-year old had a sexual relationship with the school headmaster. Although it is not clear who seduced who, the incident seemed to teach young Zelle the power she could have over men.

After being expelled from the school, Zelle lived briefly with her uncle in The Hague. In 1895, she answered a "lonely hearts" advertisement in the newspaper from Captain Rudolph McLeod, a Dutch Army officer who had been stationed in the East Indies for the past 16 years and was now on leave in Holland. The attraction between the 18-year old Zelle and the 39-year old McLeod was instant; they were engaged after just six days and were married in July 1895, after which they both moved to the Dutch colony of Indonesia. Because McLeod was the well-off son of a minor nobleman, Zelle adopted the title of "Lady McLeod".

Things quickly went sour, however. McLeod was a drunkard with a roving eye, and his nubile young wife also enjoyed the attention she got from other young Dutch Army officers. Both accused the other of infidelity. Things fell apart when the couple's two-year old son died and their younger daughter became severely sick.

(By some accounts, the children were poisoned by a housekeeper who had a grudge against McLeod; by other versions, the children had caught congenital syphilis from their philandering father.) Shortly after returning to Holland upon McLeod's discharge in 1902, the marriage broke up, they divorced in 1906, and Zelle was left to fend for herself in The Hague.

Zelle had no education and no skills, but she soon made a living by using the one thing she did have—her dark-featured exotic good looks. Moving to Paris, the 27-year old first worked the streets as an ordinary prostitute. But she soon invented a new and more lucrative persona for herself, based on the European fascination with the far-off exotic Indonesian islands. She took the name "Mata Hari" (from a Malayan expression "Eye of The Day", referring to the sun), and spun tales of being the daughter of an Indian Hindu temple dancer who had grown up in Indonesia. She claimed to be a priestess, and would perform scandalous "sacred dances" in Paris nightclubs, which were essentially stripteases. The effect was electric. The dark-eyed beauty had one string of paramours after another, who kept her supplied with money and luxuries.

In May 1914, Mata Hari began a six-month engagement at the Metropol Club in Berlin. But when the First World War broke out in August, she found herself in a difficult position. Though Holland was officially neutral in the war, Mata Hari was viewed with suspicion, and her costumes and furs were confiscated by the German authorities. Fearing that she might be arrested or detained, she escaped back to The Hague with a wealthy Dutch businessman, who set her up in a lavish chateau.

What happened after that is still a matter of controversy amongst historians. According to the version later presented by the French prosecutors (and confirmed in 1970 by documents released from the German archives), Mata Hari was approached in 1914 by the German consul in Holland and offered a large sum of money to wheedle military information out of her many army officer lovers and pass it on to the embassy. Hari's story at her trial was that she took the money from the Germans because she needed it (the war having wrecked her dancing career), but she never intended to pass on any information. British intelligence soon compiled their own dossier on her, noting that she spoke several languages, had many French, English and German military officers as companions, and, as a neutral Dutch citizen, was in a position to travel freely and pass secret information to the Germans. Two undercover security officers were assigned to keep an eye on her. By most accounts, the investigation produced abundant evidence of a long string of lovers (one of whom, amazingly, was a high official in the British intelligence service), but found no definite proof that Mata Hari was passing secrets to the Germans.

Then in 1916, Hari was briefly detained for questioning by the British while passing through London. She now claimed that she had been approached by the French intelligence service, who asked her to feed the Germans false information and to pass German secrets on to the French. The British didn't believe her, but had no hard evidence against her, and let her go.

After this, Hari was, she claimed at her trial, sent by the French to Belgium, where she was to seduce the German military governor in an attempt to obtain secrets.

Instead, she ended up in Spain with a German intelligence officer named Kalle. According to Hari, she was extracting information from him and passing it to the French: according to the French, she was passing Entente secrets on to Kalle. She returned to Paris, where the authorities decided to test her. Through one of her paramours, the French intelligence service allowed her to learn the identity of a spy who they suspected was a double agent, passing information on to both sides. Shortly later, the agent turned up dead. The French concluded that he had been killed by the Germans as a result of the information given to them by Mata Hari, and, in February 1917, the military police arrested her, melodramatically charging her with espionage that had resulted in over 50,000 battlefield deaths.

The trial took place before a military tribunal, in secret. It lasted only two days. According to some accounts, the defense was not allowed to question any of the witnesses. The official French intelligence file on Mata Hari was sealed for 100 years, and won't be released until 2017. According to some who have claimed to have seen it, there is no hard evidence cited in the dossier to establish that the dancer actually passed any military secrets to the Germans.

Mata Hari was executed by a French firing squad on the morning of October 15, 1917.

Ota Benga: The Man in the Zoo

In 1906, the Bronx Zoo put a human being, a "pygmy" from the African Congo, on display. The incident illustrates not only the pervasive racism of the early 20th century, but also the intense religious opposition to the theory of evolution.

In 1904, the city of St Louis was selected to host that year's World Fair. It was intended to be a celebration of human progress, with displays of new technology and science, and depictions of newly-explored areas of the planet. In the first years of the 20th century, the United States was changing rapidly. The "Indian Wars" had ended less than ten years ago, and America's "Manifest Destiny", having conquered the continent, now reached overseas. The US had stepped onto the world stage in the Spanish-American War, and was now a military power which had won a fledgling empire in the Pacific and the Caribbean. Rapid advances in science had led to new technologies and machinery, which transformed the US from an agricultural economy into an industrial manufacturer and would soon lead to an economic Gilded Age. Electricity, the automobile, aviation—these new technologies would soon change the world. And the United States was the leader in this transformation.

But there was a darker undercurrent as well. Economic growth had led to an enormous wave of immigration, as massive numbers of people from Europe and Asia flooded into the US to feed the insatiable American industrial machine with the hordes of low-wage workers that it needed to operate. These immigrants—from Italy, Ireland, Eastern Europe, and China—brought with them their own cultural practices, religious beliefs, and political ideologies. The white Anglo-Saxon Protestant culture in the United States viewed the newcomers as threats to their traditional way of life. Less than 50 years before, they had fought a civil war to defend the institution of slavery, then fought a cultural war to keep the newly-freed slaves "in their place". Now, they found a new target. Groups like the KKK swelled in numbers, waging a war on behalf of "the white race" against African-Americans, foreign immigrants, Catholicism, Jews, socialism, trade unionism, and anything else they viewed as "anti-American".

When the planners of the St Louis World's Fair decided that they would display an exhibit of "peoples of the world", they stepped firmly into the American culture wars. In 1859, British naturalist Charles Darwin had proposed the scientific theory of evolution, which concluded that all living things, including humans, had evolved from earlier and simpler life forms. The effect was explosive. The Protestant-Christian religion was one of the fundamental pillars of traditional Anglo-Saxon culture, in both England and the United States—the idea that God had blessed the white race and that its dominant position in the world was due, literally, to Divine Favor. When the science of evolution kicked that prop out from under them, the reaction was swift and hostile.

But the science of the time, ironically, was just as imperial and racist. Because humans had evolved, the reasoning went, it was logical to assume that different humans were more or less evolved than others. And so anthropologists of the time spent a lot of effort ranking the various races in their "evolutionary development". The black Africans, only recently freed from slavery in the US and conquered and colonized by Europeans in Africa, were placed at the bottom of the human ladder. They were "less evolved", more apelike, not quite fully human. The Asians, including the nearly-exterminated Native Americans, were a bit more "advanced". But at the top, the pinnacle of humanity, were the white

Europeans and their American cousins. They had earned their rightful place as rulers of the world not because God had willed it, but because they were biologically superior, more highly evolved, the winners in the Darwinian struggle. They were the master race.

It was under these circumstances that the St Louis World's Fair designed its exhibition of "peoples of the world". Although it was presented as science, as an illustration of various world cultures and how other people lived, the underlying message was part and parcel of the theme of the Fair as a whole—the superiority of American culture, particularly *white* American culture.

The World's Fair dispatched a number of people to gather up some natives to display, along with their traditional housing and cultural items, in what would today be called a "living history" exhibit. Members of several different Native American tribes were brought to St Louis, including the famed Apache war leader Geronimo, released from his military prison by a special order from the Secretary of War. Groups of Inuit "Eskimos" were also brought in from Alaska, as well as natives from the recently-conquered Hawaii, Samoa, and the Philippine Islands. There were native Patagonians from South America, and Ainu from northern Japan. It was, in essence, a human zoo.

Fair officials also dispatched Samuel Verner, an anthropologist and missionary who spoke several native languages, to Africa to gather some natives. In the Belgian Congo, Verner happened upon a slave trader who was selling some "pygmies"—survivors of raids by the colonial government's *Force Publique* militia. One of these captives was a member of the Mbuti tribe named

Ota Benga, whose wife and children had been killed in a raid. Verner bought him for a pound of salt and some cloth. Ota Benga and a dozen or so other Africans reached America in June 1904 and were put on display in St Louis.

The collection of natives from around the world was an immediate sensation, attracting large crowds to the Fair. With his short stature and his unusual teeth—filed down to points in the traditional Mbuti manner—Ota Benga was a particular favorite. Several newspaper accounts of the Fair mention him by name, with the *New York Times* commenting that his filed teeth were "worth the five cents he charges for showing them".

When the World's Fair ended after almost a year, the natives were all returned to their homelands. Verner accompanied the Africans back to the Belgian Congo, where he stayed in a village with the Batwa tribe and planned to do some animal collecting. Ota Benga had by this time developed a friendship with Verner, and decided to stay with him, working as his assistant and marrying a Batwa woman (who shortly later died from a snakebite). When Verner returned to the US in August 1906, Ota Benga went with him.

The American Museum of Natural History, in New York City, agreed to take Verner's collection of African animals while he traveled across the country on a lecture tour to raise money. And because Verner could not take Ota Benga with him, the museum also agreed to let the African live in a spare room inside the museum. Things did not go well. With Verner away, Ota Benga (who spoke no English) was isolated and alone, and grew increasingly sullen and hostile. Upon his return to New York, Verner tried to negotiate a deal with the Museum, in which his animals would be placed on exhibit and he would be hired to curate them. But the deal fell through, and Verner had to find another place to house his animals (and Ota Benga).

Verner then contacted the Bronx Zoo. The Zoo, opened just eight years earlier, was run by the New York Zoological Society, under its Secretary Madison Grant. The Director was William Hornaday. In the zoo world, Hornaday was a visionary: in contrast to the iron-bar prison cells that most zoos utilized to hold their animals, Hornaday was an advocate of open-air naturalistic enclosures that mimicked, as much as possible, their natural habitat. Hornaday and Grant were also enthusiastic supporters of the theory of evolution. And, perhaps inevitably, of the scientific racism that grew out of it. (Grant in particular would go on to become a prominent member of the "eugenics" movement, which advocated a program of planned breeding and sterilizations to produce evolutionarily superior humans—which won him a letter of admiration in the 1930's from German Chancellor Adolf Hitler.) Hornaday agreed to take Verner's collection of African animals for display, and also to allow Ota Benga to live at the zoo and help with the animals. (The zoo would later refer to Ota Benga as an "employee", but he was in fact never paid.)

It was then that the strangest part of the story began.

Ota Benga was given a place to sleep in a spare room and was given free run of the zoo. In particular, he liked to help the keepers with the African elephants and with the great apes in the Monkey House. During his work, he developed a bond with an orangutan named Dohong (there are no orangutans in Africa, and Ota Benga had never seen one before), and began spending several hours a day in the Monkey House.

The zoo visitors, in turn, were intrigued by the site of an African native interacting with the apes, and Hornaday realized that he had a potential crowd-draw on his hands. He encouraged Ota Benga to spend more time in the Monkey House. Over several weeks, the African moved his hammock into Dohong's cage and began to sleep there. He was then given a set of bow and arrows and spent some time each day shooting at a target. Parrots were added to the Monkey House to give it more of a "jungle" flavor, and several bones were scattered around the floor (including, it was reported, some human bones, to give a tantalizing hint of cannibalism). The visitors were delighted. So was Hornaday. One weekend a new sign appeared in the Monkey House: "The African Pigmy, 'Ota Benga.' Age, 23 years. Height, 4 feet 11 inches. Weight, 103 pounds. Brought from the Kasai River, Congo Free State, South Central Africa, by Dr. Samuel P. Verner. Exhibited each afternoon during September." Visitorship soared to 40,000 per day as curious New Yorkers lined up to see the unusual spectacle.

But the "man in the zoo" sparked immediate outrage and controversy, led mostly by the local New York African-American community. A letter to the press noted, "The person responsible for this exhibition degrades himself as much as he does the African. Instead of making a beast of this little fellow, we should be putting him in school for the development of such powers as God gave him." African-American clergyman Rev James Gordon added, "Our race, we think, is depressed enough, without exhibiting one of us with the apes. We think we are worthy of being considered human beings, with souls."

But it was not solely the open racism of the zoo exhibit that provoked opposition: many religious organizations protested because the display was seen as an endorsement of the theory of evolution. Rev Gordon declared, "The Darwinian theory is absolutely opposed to Christianity, and a public demonstration in its favor should not be permitted."

Hornaday, meanwhile, seemed rather baffled by all the opposition. In a letter to the Mayor, he wrote that he had only wanted to put "Dr. Verner's very interesting little African where the people of New York may see him without annoyance or discomfort to him." The *New York Times*, meanwhile, reflected, in an editorial, the common (racist) understanding of the time: "The pygmies ... are very low in the human scale, and the suggestion that Benga should be in a school instead of a cage ignores the high probability that school would be a place from which he could draw no advantage whatever. The idea that men are all much alike except as they have had or lacked opportunities for getting an education out of books is now far out of date."

But the organized opposition had its effect: within two weeks the offending sign was taken down, Ota Benga was banned from the Monkey House, and soon Verner was contacted and asked to find another place to house the African. Ota Benga was placed in the custody of Rev James Gordon, the same African-American pastor who had objected to his exhibition. He was first placed in the Howard Colored Orphan Asylum. After a time, he was sent to a foster family in Lynchburg VA, where his pointed teeth were capped, he went to a baptist school to learn English, and he changed his name to "Otto Bingo". He got a job working in a tobacco warehouse. At one point he was tutored in English by the local poet Anne Spencer, and through her was introduced to Booker T Washington and WEB DuBois.

By this time, however, "Otto Bingo" had seen enough of American society, and what he wanted most was to go home to the Congo. He began saving money to buy passage back to Africa.

But in 1914, the First World War broke out, and passenger ship traffic between North America and Africa came to a halt. As the war dragged on, it must have seemed to him that he would never be able to return home. In March 1916, Ota Benga walked into a patch of woods, chipped the caps off his teeth, made a ceremonial fire, and shot himself with a stolen pistol.

Pennsylvania's Roswell: The Keckburg Flying Saucer

In 1965, just a few weeks before Christmas, people in the little town of Kecksburg PA, not far from Pittsburgh, reported seeing something crash to earth from outer space. According to the stories, the US military then appeared and spirited the object away. Some whispered that it was a crashed Soviet intelligence satellite, or an American test of a secret Nazi project. Others declared it was an extraterrestrial spaceship. But what was it really....?

Here is the story of the Keckburg Flying Saucer, as usually given (with some variations) in UFO websites and books:

On December 9, 1965, witnesses all over the eastern US reported seeing a glowing object in the sky which, some of them noted, "appeared to be under intelligent control". The glowing object passed over Detroit, dropped pieces of hot metal that started grass fires in Ohio, and caused a sonic boom in Pittsburgh. At about 4:45pm, Kecksburg resident Frances Kalp called a local radio station and talked to reporter John Murphy, and told him that she had seen a glowing four-pointed object impact into a patch of woods by her house. Murphy in turn, thinking it may have been an airplane crash, called the Pennsylvania State Police.

Several local residents, meanwhile, had gathered at the crash site. They saw a bronze-colored metallic object, several feet in diameter and about ten feet high, shaped something like an acorn with a rounded top and a band around the bottom that bore an inscription written in "hieroglyphics". It was half-buried in the ground from the force of the crash. A couple of residents took photos.

When the State Police arrived, they cordoned off the area, then called in the US military. The Air Force and Army arrived. The first thing they did was confiscate all the cameras from people taking photos of the object, and threaten everyone to keep quiet about what they had seen. Then they gathered up all the wreckage and took it away on a flatbed truck, taking it to Wright-Patterson Air Force Base near Dayton OH. The official announcement was made that, after a thorough search of the woods, nothing had been found or recovered.

Since then, there have been three different versions of "what was really found at Kecksburg". One group of enthusiasts has concluded, based on the reported shape and size of the object, that it was a secret American test of advanced Nazi technology known as "*Die Glocke*" ("The Bell"). According to this story, The Bell was a secret German military project undertaken by the SS in a desperate attempt to win the Second World War by developing a super-weapon. In some versions of the story, The Bell released huge amounts of radiation that killed anyone within range. In other tales, The Bell was a device to make wormholes for space travel, or a time machine. According to this story, the Americans were testing their own version of *Die Glocke* in the woods near Kecksburg, when something went wrong, the secret test was discovered by local residents, and the military covered it up. There is of course no evidence that any such thing was ever made or conceived by anyone, much less by the Nazis, but it remains a popular tale among conspiracy-theory fans.

Another popular version of "the truth about Kecksburg" was that the object was a secret Soviet space launch that had crashed. In 1965, the manned Soyuz spacecraft, which was shaped like a bell, was in development. According to some UFOlogists, the Kecksburg incident resulted when a secret Russian test-flight of the Soyuz failed during launch and crash-landed in Pennsylvania, where the US eagerly snapped it up to study its technological secrets. In some versions, this launch was actually manned by a Russian cosmonaut test pilot who died in the crash—some accounts adding the detail that the spaceship's power was provided by a small nuclear generator with poor shielding, allowing radiation to kill the cosmonaut.

This story, oddly enough, has a tiny kernel of truth to it: the Soviets had indeed launched a space vehicle over two weeks previously. Cosmos 96 was an unmanned probe that was being sent to study Venus. It failed to reach a proper orbit when the booster rocket malfunctioned, and after 16 days in a low orbit the probe burned up upon re-entering the atmosphere on December 9. However, NASA and the US Air Force were both tracking the spacecraft by radar, and the data shows that Cosmos 96 entered atmosphere at 3:18am over Canada. It never got anywhere near Pennsylvania, and it had already burned up and disappeared by the time the Pennsylvania crash was reported at 5pm, 14 hours later.

The "Russian spacecraft" theory got a boost in 2005, however, when somebody at NASA announced that the agency had studied metal fragments from Kecksburg and concluded they were from a Soviet satellite. But nobody has been able to produce either the fragments or any reports about them, and it's likely there never were any such thing.

But by far the most popular "explanation" for Kecksburg is that it was an extraterrestrial spacecraft which had suffered some malfunction, flew over the US, and crashed in Pennsylvania. The military gathered up the wreckage, took it to Wright-Patterson's "Hangar 18" (where it presumably joined the Roswell flying saucer), and covered up the entire thing.

The Kecksburg Incident is a great story, and it still gets passed around at flying saucer and conspiracy-theory conventions, but alas, the reality was already known at the time, and is a bit less exciting....

It was known as the "Great Lakes Fireball". At 4:45pm on December 9, 1965, a brilliant meteor (known as a "bolide") was seen crossing the Great Lakes area by thousands of people in Ontario, Michigan, Ohio and Pennsylvania. The event was studied by several astrophysicists, who published a scientific paper about it in the 1967 *Journal* of the Royal Astronomical Society of Canada. Using photographs of the meteor taken by witnesses, they were able to calculate its trajectory, which showed that the bolide had descended in a sharp downward angle while traveling from the southwest to the northeast, ending in Canada on the northern shore of Lake Erie. Since no pieces of meteorite were ever found, it was presumed that the space rock had burned up in the atmosphere before reaching the ground.

People who see bright objects in the sky almost universally tend to overestimate how close it is to them. So when the people in the Kecksburg area had seen the Great Lakes Fireball, they assumed that it was flying right over their town, despite the fact that it was actually over a hundred miles away (and several miles high in the sky). When the meteor disappeared behind some trees or a hill, it was easy for them to assume it had just crashed nearby. (They were not the only ones—others reported that the meteor had landed near them in Michigan or Ohio). In reality, there was no object over Kecksburg, nothing crashed there, and the State Police search teams found nothing because there was nothing there to find. So there is no mystery to the "Kecksburg Incident"—it was simply a large meteor that was already known and studied at the time by the scientific community.

As for the "witnesses" who reported seeing the metallic acorn object on the ground, none of their "reports" was made until thirty years later, when the TV show *Unsolved Mysteries* was producing an episode about the "Incident". There were no contemporary accounts of anyone having seen any sort of crashed object. The flying saucer fans accept the thirty-year-delayed "eyewitness accounts" simply because it tells them what they already want to believe.

Who Was Really First to the North Pole?

In 1909, two people, within a week of each other, declared to the world that they had been the first person to reach the location of the North Pole. Immediate controversy broke out, and the debate has raged ever since, revolving around charges and countercharges of fraud. So, who was really first to the North Pole?

The North Pole presents a unique challenge to explorers. Unlike the South Pole, which is located in the middle of a land mass, the North Pole is located in the polar ocean, and the only way to reach it is on the ice sheet that floats on the sea's surface. Since the ice sheet continuously breaks up and moves, there is no permanent location at the North Pole—the ice that was there one year will be miles away by the next. The only way to tell that one is actually at the Pole is by careful geographical measurement of latitude. And the only way to confirm that somebody else has been there is through a careful record of the trip, including detailed navigational data.

The first attempt to reach the North Pole was in 1827, by Royal Navy officer William E Parry. His team was forced to turn back short of their goal. Over the next 70 years over a dozen other attempts, by teams from America, Norway and Italy, all failed.

In 1907, two separate teams were planning new attempts on the Pole. Robert E Peary had already made a number of unsuccessful tries. Frederick A Cook had been a member of several of Peary's previous expeditions, but was now ready to set out on his own. Although both were Americans, the two men were very different in personality. Peary was a fame-seeker and was known to drive his team relentlessly. Cook was more of a scientist, whose interest was geological but also ethnographic—he knew several native languages and did detailed studies on the Arctic native people's cultures.

Cook left first. In June 1907, he sailed to the tiny native village of Annoatok in northern Greenland, 700 miles from the Pole, and set up his base camp there. His team was small—just Cook and nine Inuit natives. After completing their preparations, they left for the Pole in February 1908. Cook planned to follow a new route that had never been tried before, only recently found by a Norwegian mapping team. His team also followed the musk oxen feeding grounds, and were able to obtain fresh meat during their journey. To cross the stretches of open water that often resulted when the ice cracked, they carried a collapsible boat with them.

At the halfway point in March, the support team turned back, as planned. The final dash to the Pole would be made by Cook and two Inuit natives.

According to Cook, the team reached the Pole at about noon on April 21, 1908, and confirmed their position with sextant readings. They spent two days there.

Upon their return, however, they ran into trouble. They had assumed that the pack ice at the Pole would be drifting eastward towards Greenland, as the ice that they had traveled across did. But instead they found a westward current at the Pole, which carried them almost 100 miles away from their pre-cached supplies. The extra distance meant that they did not make it off the ice before winter set in, and they were forced to huddle in a makeshift camp from November 1908 to February 1909. They finally reached Annoatok in April.

At Annoatok, Cook found an American hunter and adventurer, Harry Whitney, who told him that, during his 14-month disappearance, the world thought that Cook had died. Whitney also told him that a team led by Peary had left Annoatok eight months ago, in August 1908, on a quest for the Pole.

Peary's team had over 50 men, and used a relay system of sleds that went ahead and deposited caches of supplies for the main party. Unlike Cook, Peary had no boat, and had to either take the long way around stretches of open water, or stop and wait for them to freeze over or close up. When they reached a point about 140 miles from the Pole, the support team turned back for Greenland. Peary went on, accompanied by four Inuit natives and by Matthew Henson. Henson, an African-American from Maryland, had been Peary's assistant on several of his expeditions. Henson spoke the Inuit language, and it was he who took care of the team members, their dogs, and their sleds. In many ways, he was the real leader of the expedition.

On April 6, 1909, according to the later accounts of Peary and Henson, they reached the Pole. Peary's version is that he had been taking detailed sextant readings and announced that they were at the Pole. He then planted an American flag in the ice. In Henson's version, he had gone on ahead of the others, and when Peary reached him and took a sextant reading, Henson jokingly said that he had been there first, and jubilantly declared, "I am standing at the top of the world!"—which, he later wrote, made Peary "hopping mad". Peary had no desire to share his glory with a Black man and four natives.

But the word had not yet gotten out. Cook was not able to make it to a town with a wireless telegraph until September 1, 1909, when he announced that he had reached the Pole. Peary made it back a week later; his announcement went out on September 7. And the argument began that has still not been settled.

Peary, who was well-funded by the National Geographic Society, began an organized campaign in the press to dispute Cook's claim. Charges and counter-charges were traded. Cook's claim was crippled when it turned out that a previous claim he had made—as the first to reach the summit of Mt McKinley (the highest peak in Alaska) was unsupported and probably fraudulent. Cook also said that he had left his original notebook and navigational data behind in Greenland—it was never found. In 1923, Cook, now working in the oil business, was convicted of fraud in a stock market scheme and sentenced to 14 years in jail. It was the final nail in the coffin for his Pole story.

But Peary had his own problems. Henson's published account declared that Peary himself had been unsure of their exact position. Analysis of the shadows in photos taken by Peary indicated that they could have been as much as 100 miles away from the Pole. Peary had taken no instruments with him to measure longitude, assuming he wouldn't need them. But critics noted that he had claimed an extraordinarily good rate of travel to the Pole, completing the trip much faster than Cook had—and that would have been difficult to do without a longitudinal measurement to insure they were traveling in a straight line due north. Suspicions arose that Peary had not actually gotten as far as the pole.

So, what's the final conclusion? Both men still have their supporters and detractors. And a sizable minority has concluded that *neither* man actually made it to the pole.

If indeed neither Peary nor Cook actually made the trip all the way to the Pole, that would leave US Navy pilot Richard Byrd as the next claimant. In May 1926, a Fokker Triplane aircraft named "Josephine Ford" took off from Norway with Floyd Bennett as pilot and Byrd as navigator. According to their log, they reached the Pole after about 8.5 hours, circled over it, and returned.

But there are questions about Byrd's claim, too. The "Josephine Ford" would have had to have been traveling extraordinarily fast to have made the round trip in just 16 hours. And suspicions were strengthened when Byrd's original flight diary was found in an archive with other papers—with several of the navigational measurements suspiciously erased out and replaced. For many historians, Byrd's claim is also suspect.

The first person to unambiguously reach the North Pole was Norwegian arctic explorer Roald Amundsen, who flew over the pole in the airship "Norge" in 1926, just a short time after Byrd's flight. Amundsen was already the first person to reach the South Pole, in 1912.

The first person to unambiguously reach the North Pole by ground was Ralph Plaisted, who led a team on snowmobiles in 1968.

Broken Arrows: America's Lost Nuclear Weapons

"Broken Arrow" is the military's code word for an accident involving a nuclear weapon. Since 1950, there have been almost three dozen acknowledged "Broken Arrow" incidents. Several times, nuclear weapons have been dropped or accidentally released near American cities.

In the early years of the Cold War, the US Air Force Strategic Air Command was on 24-hour duty, prepared to retaliate at any time to a Soviet nuclear attack. As part of their training, US Air Force bombers would make practice flights across the country and around the world, carrying nuclear weapons. For safety, the plutonium cores that triggered the nuclear explosion were removed and either stored separately in the airplane (in a metal rack known as "the birdcage") or kept on the ground. (The 2.5 ton conventional "explosive lens" assembly that imploded the bomb to set it off, however, was intact.) Later, the Strategic Air Command began putting portions of its bomber force on "airborne alert", circling in the air with live (but "safed") nuclear weapons: it was intended to protect the bombers from being caught on the ground in a surprise Russian attack.

In February 1950, a B-36 Peacemaker strategic bomber was scheduled to make a training flight, taking off from Alaska and making a mock bombing run in Texas before returning. The Peacemaker carried one Mark 4 nuclear bomb, with the plutonium core removed. As the bomber crossed over Canada, however, ice began to clog the engine carburetors, and three engines had to be shut down. As the remaining engines began to lose power, the crew realized that the plane could not make it to safety. Steering the bomber out over the Pacific Ocean, the pilot jettisoned the nuclear weapon. The Mark 4's conventional explosives detonated on impact and the bomb was destroyed. The crew then turned back over land and bailed out. Twelve of the seventeen airmen were rescued. The B-36 flew on autopilot for a short time until it crashed into a remote mountain in British Columbia.

As it turned out, 1950 was a bad year for the Air Force. The Korean War was raging, and the US had made the secret decision to move a number of atomic bombs to staging areas in Asia where they could be readied for possible use. In April, a B-29 Superfortress took off from a base in New Mexico, bound for Guam. It was carrying General Robert Travis and a number of other officers. It was also carrying a Mark 4 atomic bomb. When the plane developed engine trouble, it tried to make an emergency landing, but the landing gear was disabled. The resulting crash set off the conventional explosives inside the Mark 4, killing a number of people on the plane and on the ground, including General Travis.

Three months later, a B-50 Superfortress (a modified version of the B-29) in Ohio crashed during a training flight, and in August a B-29 failed to make an emergency landing in California. In both of these cases, the resulting fire set off the explosive lenses in the nuclear bombs they had been carrying. Then in November 1950, a USAF B-50 experienced engine failure while flying over Canada. Before making an emergency landing, the crew set their nuclear weapon to self-destruct and dropped it over the St Lawrence River in Quebec. Although the bomb did not contain a nuclear core, it was destroyed when its explosives were set off.

In May 1957, a B-36 carrying a Mark 17 hydrogen bomb was making a landing approach at a base just outside of Albuquerque NM when the bomb broke loose, tore through the bomb bay doors, and fell onto a cattle ranch. The conventional explosives went off on impact, killing one of the cows, but although the plane was carrying a plutonium core for the Mark 17, it was separated in the "birdcage" and was not inside the bomb.

Later in 1957, a C-124 cargo plane with engine trouble was forced to jettison two of the three nuclear weapons it was carrying, dropping them off the Jersey shore, and in another incident a B-47 crashed on landing in Florida, with the resulting fire detonating the explosive lenses in the nuclear bomb it carried. In both cases, the plane had also been carrying plutonium cores.

The year 1958 was also not a good one for the USAF. There were five Broken Arrows that year, including one of the most famous.

A potentially serious accident happened in January at a base in Morocco. A B-47 was taking off on a training mission carrying a nuclear weapon with its plutonium core intact and installed in the bomb, though the weapon's electrical system had been "safed". A tire blew on takeoff, the tail hit the ground, and the fuel tank caught on fire. Remarkably, the bomb's conventional explosives did not go off.

One of the best-known Broken Arrows in the US happened a month later. While conducting a mock practice bombing exercise near Savannah GA, a B-47 bomber was intercepted by an F-86 fighter who was also on a training mission. Somehow, the two planes collided in the dark, and the crew of the crippled B-47 jettisoned their weapon, a Mark 15 hydrogen bomb, just off the coast, where it fell somewhere near the mouth of the Savannah River at Tybee Island. Despite several search attempts, the bomb was never recovered.

Just a month later, another B-47 was flying over the town of Florence SC when the shackles in the bomb bay failed, and a nuclear bomb tore through the bomb bay doors and fell out of the airplane. Several people on the ground were injured when the impact triggered the bomb's explosives.

There were two incidents in November 1958. First a B-47 crashed on takeoff in Texas, with the resulting fire setting off the explosive lenses on the nuclear bomb it was carrying. Then another B-47 burned on the ground in Louisiana. This time the explosives did not detonate, though the nuclear bomb was destroyed in the fire.

Another well-known Broken Arrow happened in January 1961. A B-52 Stratofortress was flying airborne alert over the city of Goldsboro NC, with two intact but "safed" Mark 39 hydrogen bombs, when it developed a fuel leak that led to an explosion, destroying the plane. Both of the Mark 39s fell free, with one of them deploying its parachute and landing undamaged. The second bomb's parachute failed, and it broke apart on impact, scattering pieces over a wide area. The thermonuclear "second stage" of the bomb was never found, but enough of the wrecked Mark 39 was recovered for the Air Force to determine that five of the bomb's six electrical switches had been triggered, and only the manual sixth "safe" had prevented the 20-megaton nuclear explosion.

What is probably the most famous Broken Arrow incident happened in January 1966. A B-52 on airborne alert over the Mediterranean was refueling from a tanker plane for its return to the US when the two jets collided. The Stratofortress was carrying four safed B-28 hydrogen bombs, which fell near the town of Palomares, Spain. Two of the B-28s set off their explosive lenses on impact, scattering radioactive material over a large area. One of the remaining bombs was found in a streambed. The other one fell into the Mediterranean, where it was found by a local fisherman (who negotiated with the Air Force for payment of salvage rights).

The last known Broken Arrow happened in January 1968. A B-52 was flying an airborne alert over Greenland when a fire broke out, forcing the crew to make an emergency landing at the US base in Thule. The bomber crashed short of the runway. One of the four hydrogen bombs aboard set off its explosives. Two of the bombs melted right through the pack ice and fell into the arctic ocean below. One of these was found on the seafloor 11 years later; the other was never found at all.

After 1968 the Air Force ended its practice of "airborne alerts". Since then, there have been no known Broken Arrow incidents involving nuclear bombs. The last known American nuclear weapons accident happened in 1980, when a Titan II intercontinental ballistic missile in Arkansas exploded during maintenance (a mechanic dropped a wrench and punctured a fuel tank), blowing the ICBM's 9-megaton warhead completely out of the silo.

Eleven Lost Days: Switching the Calendar

In the 18th century, England (and America) changed the calendar that it had been using for almost 2000 years. In the process, eleven days were "lost". And, according to legend, there were riots as people took to the streets to demand their eleven days back.

226 - GREGORY XIII

In ancient times, most calendars were lunar, and were based on the period of time between full moons or new moons. This, however, caused a problem over the longterm. The 30-day lunar cycle did not fit evenly into the 365-day solar cycle, so after a period of years any specific dates based on lunar cycles would be falling into completely different seasons. As a result, most agricultural societies began keeping solar time instead, based on the motion of the sun in the sky; astronomical observations were carefully kept to determine the time of the spring and autumn equinoxes and the summer and winter solstices. This still caused problems, however, since the solar cycle did not equal 365 days—it actually lasts roughly 365.25 days. So the solar calendar gradually fell out of step with the actual cycle of the sun.

In the Roman times, the early calendar was divided into ten months. (September, October, November and December come from the Latin for seven, eight, nine and ten.) The days of each month were counted from the first day (the Kalends), and the middle day (the Ides). Later two more months were added. But this still left the year too short, so every so often two extra months (called the Intercalaris) had to be added. It was up to the priests to keep track of all this, and since nobody else actually understood the calendar's workings, it was not unusual for the priesthood to adjust the length of the year (sometimes through bribery), making it longer or shorter for political or religious reasons.

In 45 BCE, under the rule of Julius Caesar, the mess became so confusing that a change was needed, and the Roman Republic adopted a version of the solar calendar that became known as the "Julian". For the first time, this new calendar introduced the concept of the "leap year"—

an extra day tacked on to one of the months to correct the discrepancy caused by the fraction in the solar cycle. The Julian calendar also changed the beginning of the year. The old Roman calendar had used March 1 as the beginning of each year; the Julian system moved this to January 1.

The Julian calendar remained long after the Roman Empire collapsed. It was adopted by the Roman Catholic Church and held sway throughout Europe for the next thousand years. The only modification to be made during this time was to change the date of the first of the year. The early Church, as part of an effort to emphasize the Christian holy days instead of the pagan Roman, moved the first day of the year away from January 1. In the 7th century CE Christmas Day was the beginning of the new year; by the 9th century CE the new year was set at March 25, Annunciation Day.

However, the Julian calendar also had a problem. The solar cycle, it turned out, was not exactly 365.25 days—it was a little less than that. So by adding a leap day every four years, the Julian calendar was actually adding too much time, and it fell out of step with the actual solar cycle by one full day every 128 years. By the 16th century CE, the calendar dates were ten days out of sync with the solar equinoxes and solstices.

This was a problem for the Church. Holy days such as Easter were calculated astronomically from the solar equinoxes and the lunar phases, but these were now irreconcilable with the calendar dates (Easter had traditionally been celebrated on March 21). So in 1582, Pope Gregory XIII introduced a sweeping change to bring the calendar back into alignment with the solar cycle. He decreed that ten days would be dropped in

October; October 1 would be followed immediately by October 12. He also declared that the beginning of the new year would be moved to January 1. And finally, to solve the problems with the Julian calendar, Pope Gregory reduced the number of leap days: now instead of adding a leap day every four years, it would be added only if that year was not divisible by 400.

The Gregorian calendar went into effect in Catholic Europe in October 1582. The Protestant countries, however, flatly refused to adopt the "Popish timekeeping", and kept their Julian calendar. As a result, Europe now had two different calendars, simultaneously. To avoid confusion, civil, commercial and diplomatic documents began "double dating", listing both the Julian and Gregorian dates. (But, to make things more confusing, in 1600 Scotland, then an independent kingdom, moved the beginning of the year on its Julian calendar from March 25 to January 1. Then in 1603, King James of Scotland also became King of England, and the British Isle had the same calendar but with two different New Year's days.)

This awkward system continued for almost 150 years, but soon it became so unwieldy that it could no longer be tolerated. In 1750, England bowed to reality, and Parliament passed a resolution that implemented the Gregorian calendar to bring Britain and her colonies into sync with the rest of the world. The beginning of the year was moved from March 25 (known as Lady Day) to January 1, and eleven days were dropped (the delay in adopting the Gregorian system had allowed the Julian calendar to become inaccurate by an extra day). As a result, March 24, 1750, was followed by March 25, 1751, but December 31, 1751, was then followed by January 1,

1752. (Thus the year 1751 lasted only 282 days instead of 365, and there was no January or February in that year.) Then, on Wednesday, September 2, 1752, eleven days were dropped, and the next day became Thursday, September 14.

In later centuries, a myth appeared that the benighted English peasants, upon being told that 11 days would be dropped from the calendar, thought that their lives were actually being shortened by almost two weeks, and rioters appeared in the streets demanding their eleven days back. In reality, contemporary records show no such incidents, although there were some local protests when a few landlords tried to collect a full month's rent for the short month of September. The calendar change did become a political issue in Parliament between the Whigs and the Tories, with the conservatives opposing the "papish calendar".

A few countries, however, still retained the Julian calendar. Tsarist Russia never adopted the Gregorian system. It wasn't until the Soviet Union was established in 1917 that the new calendar came into use (which is why the February and October Revolutions happened in March and November). The last nation to adopt the Gregorian calendar was Turkey, in 1927.

Yamamoto Otokichi's Unintentional Trip Around the World

In 1832, a Japanese cargo ship with 14 people aboard was caught in a storm and pushed out into the Pacific. One of them was 14-year old Yamamoto Otokichi, who was about to begin an unexpected two-decade trip around the world.

In the year 1600, the Japanese warlord Ieyasu Tokugawa defeated his last remaining rival, unified Japan under his control, and took de facto power from the Emperor. Under the title of Shogun ("great barbarian-defeating general"), Tokugawa's rule was absolute. The only possible threat to his regime (and to the independence of Japan itself) came from the Europeans, and over the next few years, the Shogun took drastic measures. In 1606, the practice of Christianity was outlawed in Japan, and the Portuguese missionaries were all expelled. In 1636, the Shogun carried this further; he not only expelled all foreigners from Japan, but banned any Japanese people from traveling to other countries, or even building a large sea-going ship, under penalty of death. Only one port island, in Nagasaki, was left open to a small tightly-regulated trade with China, Korea, and Holland. The policy became known as *sakoku* (literally, "locking the country shut"). The Tokugawa Shoguns would rule Japan for the next 200 years, and the islands became the most isolated places in the world.

On October 11, 1832, two centuries after the Shogun's edict, the 50-foot cargo ship *Hojun Maru* set sail from the tiny coastal village of Mihama, bound for the capitol city of Edo (modern-day Tokyo) with 150 tons of rice and porcelain pottery. On the trip, the little boat was caught in one of the fierce storms that often ravaged the Japanese coast. Pounding waves broke off the mast, and the ship's rudder was torn away. When the storm ended, the *Hojun Maru* was adrift in the Pacific, out of sight of land, with neither a sail for propulsion nor a rudder for steering. The 15-man crew was completely at the mercy of wind and current.

For over a year, they drifted helplessly. They survived by eating the rice cargo and catching fish, and by modifying a sake distillery to make fresh drinking water from seawater. One thing they did not have, however, was a source of vitamin C, and one by one they began to succumb to scurvy. After 14 months, only three of the fifteen crewmen were still alive: a 29-year old sailor named Iwakichi, a 16-year old named Kyukichi, and 15-year old Yamamoto Otokichi.

Finally, in December 1833, the floating hulk of the *Hojun Maru* washed ashore. At first, the sailors thought they had drifted into one of the island groups south of Japan. But when they encountered a group of people, everything about them was different from anything the Japanese had ever heard of. The people were from a band of Native Americans known as the Makah. The crippled Japanese boat had drifted all the way across the Pacific to North America, and were now in a part of the Oregon Territory that would become the state of Washington.

The Makah, in turn, did not know what to make of these odd people who had come from the ocean. They took the castaways to one of their fishing villages and nursed them back to health, then, following the accepted customs of the Pacific Northwest tribes, they kept them as captive laborers.

Over the next few months, stories were passed from tribe to tribe about the three strangers, and eventually the tale, along with a drawing, reached Dr John McLoughlin, a British territorial official in Fort Vancouver. From the pictograph characters written on the drawing, McLoughlin concluded that the men must have come from China, and sent a naval expedition to find them. By the summer of 1834 Otokichi and his two companions were at the Fort. They were taught English by a local clergyman, and once McLoughlin was able to converse with them, he was amazed to learn that they were not Chinese, but Japanese. By this time, Japan had been completely closed to foreigners for over 200 years, and virtually nothing was known about the secretive islands.

Here, McLoughlin realized, was a unique opportunity for the British Government to make contact with the Japanese Shogun, perhaps even leading to diplomatic and trade relations and strengthening England's position in the north Pacific. In November 1834, McLoughlin sent the three Japanese castaways on the Hudson Bay Company ship *Eagle,* which was heading for England by way of Hawaii, hoping that Parliament would send a diplomatic mission along with them to Edo. Otokichi, Kyukichi and Iwakichi arrived in London in June 1835.

But the British Government was already entangled with trade disputes in China, culminating in the Opium Wars, and had no room on the agenda for Japan. Instead of sending a diplomatic mission to the Shogun, Parliament took the three Japanese sailors on a quick tour of London and then sent them to the Portuguese port of Macao in China. They were taken in by Karl Gutzlaff, a German working for the British Government as a translator. Over the next two years, the three exiles taught Japanese to Gutzlaff and helped him write a translation of the New Testament. While in Macao, the group was joined by four new Japanese sailors who had just been caught in a storm and blown to the Philippines. There was no attempt to return the castaways to Japan, apparently because they feared that, having lived for so long among the foreigners, they would be killed by the Shogun if they came back.

But in July 1837, an American merchantman, Captain Charles W King of the USS *Morrison*, appeared in Macao with plans to approach the Japanese Shogun for permission to begin trade voyages. King offered to take all seven of the castaways back to Japan, hoping to use this as a means of establishing contact with the Edo government in a gesture of goodwill. Instead, when the *Morrison* entered Edo's harbor, it was fired on by Japanese cannon. King left and tried to enter Japan again, at the port of Kagoshima, but was fired on once more. He managed to contact a local official, who took two of the seven Japanese castaways, but then told King to leave. The *Morrison* returned to Macao with Otokichi and the four others.

Now 21 years old, Otokichi decided that he would never be allowed to return to Japan, and made a life for himself in China. Moving to Shanghai, Otokichi became a translator for British and American shipping companies, married a Malay woman from Singapore and had four children, became a British citizen, and took the English name John Ottoson. He finally got a chance to visit Japan, only briefly, in 1849, when the British ship HMS *Mariner* was allowed to enter Edo harbor on a mapping expedition. Otokichi served as a translator: to hide from Japanese authorities who he feared might arrest him, he posed as the son of a Chinese businessman.

The Shogun's policy of *sakoku* finally collapsed in July 1853, when US Navy Commodore Matthew Perry led a fleet of warships into Edo and, at the point of a cannon, forced Japan to sign a treaty opening her ports to American trading ships. Other countries followed, and when the British sent a fleet to impose their own trade treaty in October 1854, Yamamoto Otokichi was there as a translator, under his British name "John Ottoson". It was 22 years, almost to the day, since the 14-year old boy had left port on the *Hojun Maru*.

During the talks, Otokichi made contact with a number of Japanese officials and was apparently issued a request by the Shogun's government to return to Japan, but Otokichi chose instead to return to his family in Shanghai. After the treaty, the British Government awarded him a large sum of money, which he used to move with his wife and children to Singapore. He died there in 1867.

How CBS Smothered the Smothers Brothers

In the late 1960's, at the height of the civil rights movement, the Vietnam War, and the hippie revolution, the Smothers Brothers Comedy Hour became the most controversial show in TV history and, despite winning an Emmy, was abruptly pulled off the air.

In the 1960's, the US was torn by a social divide that ran largely across generational lines. The civil rights movement, the women's liberation movement, and the opposition to the Vietnam War, all produced political conflict across both parties. Political rallies, mass demonstrations, campus occupations, civil rights protests—all were weekly occurrences. Young people flocked to join and support the Students for a Democratic Society (SDS), the Black Panthers, and the Yippies. The hippie counterculture brought rock music to a new level of political awareness (and volume), and celebrated the recreational use of drugs like marijuana and LSD. One popular slogan said "Don't trust anyone over 30".

But in the world of network television, the social conflicts were nearly invisible. Westerns dominated television, with such popular shows as "Gunsmoke", "Have Gun Will Travel", and "Wagon Train". The number one TV show in 1966 was "Bonanza", a western that ran on the NBC network. The competing CBS network had tried to beat "Bonanza" by moving two of its most popular shows, "Perry Mason" and "The Garry Moore Show", to the same time slot to compete with it, but both failed utterly.

In desperation, CBS tried a new approach. Rather than trying to draw away "Bonanza's" audience, they would use that time slot to bring in an entirely new audience with a different demographic. CBS was already seen as "the old folks network", appealing mainly to people 45 and over. So, to win a new younger audience, CBS wanted a show that was "hip" and "edgy" and would appeal to the members of the under-30 counterculture generation. And, CBS execs thought, they had the perfect stars for it.

Throughout the 60's, the Smothers Brothers, Tom and Dick, had been performing their comedy/music act, in which they sang folk songs and traded barbs around sibling rivalry (their signature line being "Mom liked you best!"). It was a popular stage act, and the pair had also released several successful comedy/music record albums. CBS had signed the pair to do a sitcom show a few years before, but that format did not suit their style of comedy and it quickly failed. Now, CBS was ready to let them try again, in a variety-show format which would showcase their music and comedic banter, and feature a number of guests each episode. It would be called "The Smothers Brothers Comedy Hour". It entered the CBS schedule in February 1967 as a mid-season replacement, opposite "Bonanza".

From the beginning, the show assembled some of the most talented young writers in the business. The head writer was comic/song composer Jim Stafford (who would go on to fame with his music album "Not Just Another Pretty Foot"). Other writers were Rob Reiner (who would shortly go on to star in the groundbreaking sitcom "All in the Family"), Don Novello (later famous as "Father Guido Sarducci"), Bob Einstein (who later became "Super Dave Osbourne"), Pat Paulsen (who would run a comedic electoral campaign in 1968 for President of the United States), and, in his first TV job, future comedy superstar Steve Martin.

In the first season, "The Smothers Brothers Comedy Hour" was relatively conservative. The premiere featured guests Jill St John and Jim Nabors, with the Brothers being introduced by Ed Sullivan. Later guests included Bette Davis, Jack Benny, Kate Smith, George Burns, and Jimmy Durante. But over time the acts became younger and edgier, and the satire became more openly political. Youth-oriented rock bands like Steppenwolf, Jefferson Airplane, Cream, Simon and Garfunkel, and The Doors played sets. African-American artists like Diahann Carroll and civil rights activist/calypso singer Harry Belafonte were invited to appear—which upset CBS affiliate stations in the segregationist South. The band Buffalo Springfield performed their antiwar song "For What It's Worth". A series of skits titled "Share a Little Tea With Goldie" featured comedian Leigh French as hippie chick "Goldie O'Keefe" in a parody of radio call-in advice shows. Apparently the network execs never figured out that the entire skit was a celebration of recreational drug use: "tea" was counterculture slang for "marijuana", and "Goldie" answered phone calls with "Hi...and glad I am."

In December 1967, folk singer Pete Seeger, a former Communist Party member who had been blacklisted by McCarthy's House Un-American Activities Committee back in the 50's, was invited to sing his antiwar song "Waist Deep in the Big Muddy": the segment was axed by the network. Another sketch series on the show featured comedian David Steinberg as a pastor delivering a wickedly satirical short sermon: CBS ordered that the skits be pulled, calling them "sacrilegious". In one opening sketch, Tom Smothers declared that he could tell people apart by the amount of clothing they wear. The common people, he said, were the less-ons, and the rich people were the more-ons. And when asked by Dick who was running the country, Tom grinned at the camera and answered, "The morons".

CBS's CEO and President, William S Paley, was a personal friend of President Lyndon Johnson, and Johnson had been leaning on Paley to curb the satirical attacks against his policies being made on the show. CBS now demanded that all of the taped episodes be submitted several weeks before airing so they could be "edited for content". In response, the show turned its fire against CBS itself. Comedian Pat Paulsen, who was now running a tongue-in-cheek campaign for President of the United States, did a "press conference" on the show denouncing censorship. Guest star Elaine May did a sketch in which she and Tom Smothers played TV censors who were reviewing a show—which was then itself censored by CBS. This led to Tom and Dick waving a copy of the banned script on camera, declaring that they were being "shut up by CBS".

The show had such high ratings, particularly among younger audiences, that it finished the year ranked number 12 in the nation, and was renewed for a second and then a third season, but both the writers and the performers continued to clash with CBS censors. When The Who appeared during the second season to play their counterculture anthem "My Generation", they finished the show, literally, with a bang. The band had a tradition of ending their stage concerts by smashing their equipment: Pete Townsend would pound his guitar on the floor, and Keith Moon would set off small explosive charges inside his drum set. During the taping of their TV performance, however, a much larger explosive charge was accidentally loaded, and it detonated with a blast of smoke that pushed singer Roger Daltrey almost off the stage, dropped flaming sparks onto Pete Townsend's hair, and peppered Keith Moon's arms with shrapnel.

Harry Belafonte taped a performance of the song "Lord, Don't Stop the Carnival" while standing in front of filmed scenes of police beating protesters at the 1968 Chicago Democratic Party Convention. CBS cut the entire segment, leaving the show five minutes short—which they filled with paid Nixon campaign ads. During the third season, folk singer Joan Baez dedicated her performance to her husband, who had just been jailed for resisting the draft. CBS pulled the entire show and replaced it on air with a rerun. After protests about the censorship, the show was aired later, with Baez's statement edited out.

But the "Smothers Brothers Comedy Hour" continued to be a ratings hit, and won an Emmy for Best Writing in a Comedy Series. In March 1969, it was announced that the show had been contracted for a fourth season.

It was not to be. CBS CEO William Paley personally ordered that the show not be renewed. The network announced the cancellation on April 4. The reason given was that the brothers had not been submitting their taped shows in time for "review" prior to airing. One remaining show had already been taped, but was now never aired.

The unilateral cancellation provoked a storm of criticism, with even the *New York Times* condemning the censorship. The Smothers Brothers sued CBS, declaring that it had breached their contract by canceling the show after already agreeing to a fourth season. They eventually won and were awarded some $900,000, but "The Smothers Brothers Comedy Hour" was gone. The brothers took their show (minus the political satire) to both NBC and ABC over the next few years, but without its edgy humor it never got the ratings that the original did.

In the 1990's, the E! Network aired old episodes of the Smothers Brothers show, intercut with interviews of cast members explaining the controversies and censorship battles. And in 2002 a documentary, "Smothered", aired on the Bravo Network which explored the show's battles and eventual cancellation by CBS.

Today, the whole incident is presented in film school classrooms as a textbook example of censorship and the creative conflicts between artists and media executives. And it is studied by social scientists as a way of understanding the political and cultural conflicts of the 1960's.

The Crystal River Nuclear Power Plant: How Progress Energy Broke its Own Nuke

In 2009, the Progress Energy company in Tampa Bay FL decided to upgrade its aging nuclear power plant at Crystal River by replacing the plant's steam generators with newer ones. This was a routine operation that had already been done in several dozen other nukes around the US. But in the case of Crystal River, it turned out to be anything but routine.

The Crystal River Unit 3, located in rural Citrus County FL near the Gulf of Mexico, was one of the last nuclear power stations to be built in the United States, being completed in 1976. The 860 MW pressurized-water reactor was the only nuclear-powered plant at what would over the years become a 5-unit power station, one of the largest in the US. (The other four units were all coal-fired.)

But by 2009, Crystal River Unit 3, like all the other nuclear plants in the US, had been in service for over 30 years, and was reaching the end of its designed lifespan. To keep the aging nukes running, electric companies across the US had begun upgrading some of the equipment to give them another 20 years or so of useful life.

In September 2009, Unit 3 was scheduled for a routine shut-down to have its nuclear fuel replaced, and Progress Energy had already decided to use the opportunity to replace the 30-year old steam generators with new ones, which would increase the lifespan of the plant and also increase its electricity output by about 20%. Since the generators were located inside the thick concrete containment building that surrounded the nuclear reactor (which was designed to prevent radioactive contamination if there were an accident) and were too big to fit through the existing door, the procedure for replacing them involved cutting a large hole, some 30x20 feet, through the thick wall, and using the hole to gain access. While this might sound drastic, it had already been done over a dozen times before in the US and was a rather routine task. It was expected that the work would be finished and the plant would be up and running again by December.

But when workers began to cut the hole through the containment wall, they noticed some places where the wall had cracked and the concrete had "de-laminated"—the several layers of concrete that made up the wall had separated from each other, and large patches of the inner wall were flaking off in huge chunks. Further probing discovered that the cracked and damaged area was extensive—it was apparent that the wall had essentially been destroyed, and the entire containment building would have to be torn down and rebuilt. The cost was estimated at over $2.5 billion. Progress Energy assumed that its insurance would cover most of the costs.

But here is where things started to get strange.....

Years before, the Florida State Legislature had passed a law called the "Nuclear Cost Recovery Act". In effect, the law stated that an electric company that wanted to build a nuclear power plant could go to the Public Service Commission, the governing body that oversaw Florida's utilities, and ask permission to begin charging its customers an increased rate, raising their electric bills to pay for the costs. Not only could this be done before the plant was even begun, but if, for any reason, the nuke never got built, there was no obligation for the company to give back any of the money. Further, although the electric company was a privately-owned for-profit Fortune 500 company, as a state-sanctioned monopoly it was granted a guaranteed Return On Investment, and the surcharges already contained the electric company's built-in ROI.

In effect, the company's customers would not only be paying the cost of the nuke, but also paying the company's profits, before any shovels were put into the ground—and the public would continue paying even if the nuke were never actually built. It was a sweetheart deal, and its passage may or may not have had something to do with the fact that for many years the top three campaign contributors in Florida's state legislature races were all electric companies, two of which had plans to build new nuclear stations.

So when the upgrade to Crystal River 3 went bust (literally), Progress Energy went to the Public Service Commission and asked to have consumers pay whatever amount of the $2.5 billion that its insurance didn't cover. And as part of the process, the PSC began an investigation into the circumstances of the accident. They did not expect to find what they found. Progress Energy's story was that they had been doing a routine job when all of sudden, quite unexpectedly and unpredictably, the wall just ... well ... *broke*. They had no idea at all, by golly, how or why it happened. But the investigation quickly found that Progress was being less than forthcoming, and the company's own internal memos, emails and files revealed the true story.

By the time Progress Energy decided to upgrade its nuke, the same operation had already been done 34 times in other plants in the US, and in 13 of those cases, it had been necessary to cut through the containment building to replace the generators. All of those jobs had been carried out by one of just two companies, Bechtel Corporation or SGT. They all went without a hitch.

At the time it first decided to replace the generators, back in 2004, Progress Energy approached SGT to do the work. The job would cost a total of $230 million, of which about $81 million would go for SGT's management fees. But then, someone in Progress Energy's upper-level management had what they apparently thought was a great idea—if they bypassed SGT entirely, managed the project themselves, and hired Bechtel solely to do the actual construction work, they could save the company somewhere between $15 and $30 million.

The idea drew immediate criticism within the company. An internal memo pointed out that "large scale engineering and construction management is not our core business", and others argued that the company's inexperience in overseeing this type of project could very likely cause lots of delays that would ultimately swamp out any savings.

Nevertheless, Progress Energy decided to go ahead with the "do-it-yourself" management plan. It hired Bechtel to do the actual work on replacing the generators, and another company called Mac & Mac Hydrodemolition (which had never worked on a nuclear plant) to cut the actual hole through the wall. To do all the preliminary planning, Progress hired an engineering company called Sargent and Lundy, which had never worked on a steam generator replacement before. These all agreed to work directly under Progress's management.

During the planning, Progress continuously pushed Sargent and Lundy to do things on the cheap. Nuclear containment buildings are built from concrete which is reinforced by a number of tightened steel bands, called "tendons". The Crystal River plant had 426 tendons. In the process of cutting through the wall, a number of these tendons had to be loosened (called "de-tensioning"). When Sargent and Lundy submitted its plans for the project, they called for a total of 97 of the tendons to be loosened. Progress Energy management in turn complained that "de-tensioning the tendons is a very expensive and time-consuming effort," and asked S&L to reduce the "excessive" number.

The next proposal was for 74 tendons to be loosened—about the same number as had been done in all the other plants that had undergone the procedure. It still wasn't enough to satisfy Progress. Company execs told Sargent and Lundy to "put their thinking caps on" and find "an alternative method . . . that would result in a lot less tendons being de-tensioned". S&L returned with a proposal to loosen just 65 tendons—lower than any of the other projects. Progress Energy, delighted with the cost savings, accepted the plan.

But in September 2009, when the actual work began, it quickly became apparent that there were additional unusual things being proposed, apparently to save time and costs. In order to keep the tension evenly distributed around the containment building, it was necessary to loosen the tendons in a staggered pattern. Progress Energy management, however, was ordering the Bechtel workers to de-tension the tendons sequentially, right next to each other. The normal procedure was also to loosen all the necessary tendons before attempting to cut the actual hole through the wall; Mac and Mac was being ordered to begin cutting the hole after only 27 tendons had been loosened. A number of the Bechtel supervisors had worked on the projects at the other nuclear plants, and they were concerned at these departures from standard operating procedure. "I have never heard of it being done like this before," noted one foreman in a memo to his boss, "and I just want to express my concerns to you one last time." Bechtel's project supervisor asked in an email, "Why are we doing tendons different here than all other jobs?" Progress

Energy responded with a bland, "I am satisfied the Sargent & Lundy approach is technically correct and will withstand scrutiny."

The cutting process began in October 2009. Within an hour, cracks appeared in the wall of the containment building. Soon "large chunks" were popping loose and falling out. The work was halted. The company's efforts to save itself $15 million had resulted in the destruction of a $2.5 billion building.

The Public Service Commission's investigation concluded, as did the Nuclear Regulatory Commission's later, that it was the non-standard procedure followed by Progress Energy, particularly in loosening all the tendons in sequence in the same area, that caused the tension to become uneven and cracked the wall. Not only was Progress's excuse that "no one could have predicted this" rejected, but their own documentation showed that it *had* indeed been predicted by its own workforce. Within a short time, Progress Energy's insurance company, apparently having reached the same conclusion, informed the company management that it would not be paying any of the repair costs. Progress nevertheless asked the PSC to allow the company to charge its customers an extra $50 per month, on average, to pay to fix the nuke they had just broken.

A flurry of lawsuits and regulatory complaints from PE customers followed. The local Occupy Wall Street group ("Occupy St Pete") made the Crystal River situation one of its primary projects, arguing that it was corporate welfare at its worst. They organized protest rallies at the Progress Energy corporate headquarters, appeared on local radio and newspapers, and began to coordinate an effort with other state groups to begin a referendum process to repeal the entire "Nuclear Cost Recovery" policy.

At the same time, a number of lawsuits appeared over Progress Energy's plans to build two new nuclear power plants in Levy County FL. These had originally been budgeted at $7 billion, but the cost had already tripled to over $20 billion, and construction had yet to begin. It was widely expected by industry experts that the final cost for the two nukes would be at minimum between $25 and $30 billion, making them the most expensive nuclear power plants ever built. And despite the fact that the permits had not even been issued yet, Progress had already charged its consumers some $1.5 billion towards the Levy plants, which included its own built-in ROI of around 8%. The soaring costs made it increasingly more likely that the two nukes would in fact never be built at all—in which case Progress Energy would get to keep all the money it had already collected from its customers. Lawsuits were filed challenging the "cost recovery".

And in the middle of all this, in 2012, Progress Energy was bought by Duke Energy, which became the largest electric company in the US—and which inherited all of Progress's difficulties with the Crystal River and Levy County nukes.

In the end, it all played out much as industry experts had expected it would. Duke Energy announced that it would shut down and dismantle the Crystal River Unit 3 instead of repairing it. In a settlement deal with the PSC to end all the lawsuits, Duke agreed to refund over $380 million to consumers that it had already collected for the wrecked Crystal River plant, but consumers would still be on the hook for about $3.2 billion towards the Levy County nukes, plus future costs. Not long after this agreement, Duke cancelled the two new nuclear plants, citing the skyrocketing costs (which it now estimated at almost $25 billion). The Florida legislature, stung by the way its Nuclear Cost Recovery law backfired, ordered that a review of the policy be undertaken when it expires in 2017, and both Duke and the PCS agreed not to charge customers for the two cancelled nukes until after that review is completed.

Decommissioning the Crystal River nuke is currently expected to cost about $1.2 billion, and take about sixty years.

Earth's Other Moons

If someone were to ask you "how many moons does the Earth have?", you would answer "One". And you would be correct—most of the time. But not all of the time.....

When it comes to moons in our solar system, Earth is kind of an oddball. Most of the planets have a number of moons. Jupiter and Saturn, the gravitational powerhouses among our planets, have over 60 each. Uranus has almost 30, and Neptune has around 15. Mars has 2, and Pluto has 5. Mercury and Venus have none.

Earth's moon, Luna, is unique in several ways. Nearly all of the other moons in our solar system are actually asteroids (or in the case of Pluto, Neptune, and Uranus, Kuiper Belt objects) that wandered too close to a planet, were captured by gravity, and became locked in orbit. Our Moon, however, is the result of a chance encounter, billions of years ago when there were many more planets circling the Sun than there are today. At that time, Earth shared its orbit with a Mars-sized fellow planet, now called Thea, and when they collided, a large chunk of the Earth's mantle was blown off into space, settled into orbit around us, and eventually coalesced to form the Moon. As a result of its unusual birth, our Luna has one of the largest sizes relative to the planet that it orbits than any other moon in the solar system—only Pluto's moon Charon has a higher ratio.

From the 1840's to the 1960's, there were around half a dozen claims from people, some of them professional astronomers, who declared they had observed small moons, up to 400 miles across, in orbit around the Earth. One of these was even given the proposed name "Lilith". But none of these observations was ever confirmed. In the 1950's, the US Air Force began one of the first searches for Near-Earth Asteroids which had the potential to collide with us. Astronomer Clyde Tombaugh, who had recently discovered Pluto, ran the project. Flying saucer "investigator" Donald Keyhoe produced a series of magazine articles claiming that the project had secretly discovered one or two small moons orbiting the Earth at about 300 miles altitude, but had covered up the find (presumably because the space aliens had a UFO base there). Tombaugh had to make a number of announcements that no new Earth moonlets had been found.

For many years, the fact that Earth had only one Moon—and it was not a captured asteroid—was something of a puzzle. Venus and Mercury were close to the Sun in a zone where there aren't many asteroids, so it was no surprise that they had no moons. But Earth's orbit is criss-crossed by a fairly large number of asteroids, and it seemed odd that none of them had been captured by our planet's gravity to become a second moon. Mathematical models and computer simulations often had Earth capturing passing asteroids and holding them in orbit at least temporarily. The three-body gravitation of the Sun, Earth, and Luna made them unstable, however, and they would always, sooner or later, be perturbed and ejected from Earth orbit. According to these models, Earth should have a virtually continuous (on the galactic time scale) traveling companion, as asteroids, ranging in size from several feet to several miles, would be grabbed by gravity, orbit for a time before being kicked away, then be replaced by another. Astronomers began to refer to them as "mini-moons".

Then, it was announced that indeed such a "temporary mini-moon" had been found. Back in September 2006 a team from the University of Arizona noticed an object in a very slow polar orbit around the Earth. Measuring around 15 feet long (about the size of a typical midsize car), it was at first thought to be just an empty piece of the Saturn V rocket that took one of the Apollo spaceships to the Moon, but calculations of its mass showed it to be a rocky asteroid. It was given the designation RH120. Just 13 months after it was first detected, while at the farthest point in its orbit, the mini-moon was perturbed by gravitational forces and was ejected from Earth orbit, to once again become just another tiny Near-Earth Asteroid sweeping around the Sun. But our little mini-moon will return—calculations show that RH120's orbit brings it into an approach to Earth every 22 years, close enough to probably be captured. The next close approach will be in August 2028, when we will likely have another temporary second moon.

Indeed, astronomers have now found that in the game of gravity wells, nothing is permanent, and all sorts of odd things can go on. Mars currently has two moons, Phobos and Deimos. These are captured asteroids. But the orbit of the larger moon, Phobos, is decaying, and in about ten million years (a mere eyeblink on the galactic time scale) it will crash into the planet, and Mars will have only one moon. Many of the moons of Jupiter and Saturn are also just temporary visitors: they will either be kicked out of orbit to wander around the Sun on their own, or will be drawn in and crushed inside the gas giants. In the Kuiper Belt, where there are a large number of small objects interacting with each other, gravitational captures are virtually inevitable. Neptune's large moon Triton revolves in a "backwards" orbit around the planet compared to the planet's other moons, indicating that it is probably a captured Kuiper Belt object. Pluto's largest moon Charon is almost half its own diameter, an example of a Kuiper Belt object being captured by another Kuiper Belt object.

So far, there have been no observed examples of a moon orbiting a moon which itself orbits a planet. Such a three-tier system is entirely possible, though the complex gravitational interactions would make it unstable and temporary. In January 2016, measurements of gravitational disturbances in the orbits of Kuiper Belt objects led a team of astronomers to conclude that there must be another large planet orbiting the sun, beyond Pluto, which is causing those perturbations. The hunt began to find the predicted "Planet X".

In addition to its temporary little "mini-moon" traveling companions, Earth has a number of odd objects in nearby space, some of which have been (incorrectly) called "second moons".

In October 1986, a Scottish researcher working in Australia found a near-Earth asteroid measuring about three miles across, and named it 3753 Cruithne, after an ancient Irish king. As with all near-Earth objects, Cruithne's orbit was measured to see if it presented any collision danger. But instead of a simple smooth ellipse, the asteroid's orbit was pushed and pulled so much by gravitational interactions that its complex path was not fully calculated until 1997. Cruithne's orbit was incredibly convoluted, with a pattern that sometimes brought it close to Mars and sometimes to Venus. From our point of view on Earth, over a period of 770 years the asteroid appears to move almost completely around the night sky, then suddenly stop and go almost completely around in the other direction before reversing again—a phenomenon known as a "horseshoe orbit". But the odd part is that Cruithne, despite its wobblings and wanderings, takes almost exactly the same amount of time to orbit the Sun as Earth does. The press dubbed it "our second moon", but that label is not correct, since Cruithne orbits the Sun, not the Earth. But its odd synchronized pathway around our planet has earned it the label "quasi-orbital satellite". Since then, similar Sun-centered "quasi-satellites" have been found around Mars, Jupiter, and Saturn, and two more around the Earth.

Like most asteroids, Cruithne's orbit is not stable. Some calculations seem to suggest that in roughly 8,000 years, the asteroid will approach Venus—not close enough to be captured, but perhaps enough to "slingshot" around the planet and be accelerated, likely being tossed out beyond Mars.

Another odd asteroid was discovered in 2010. Called TK7, it is a nondescript space rock about 1000 feet long—the size of an aircraft carrier. What makes it unusual is its location: at some time in the past, the asteroid happened to move through a "Lagrange point"—a mathematical location where the gravitational pull of the Earth, the Moon and the Sun are all equally balanced by centrifugal force. TK7 is lodged in Lagrange Point 4, just ahead of the Earth in its orbit. Calculations indicate that it may have been caught in the L4 point for some 1500 years. Similar Lagrange satellites were already seen near Mars, Jupiter, Neptune, and some of Saturn's moons. Such asteroids are now given the name "Trojans". Since they do not actually orbit their planet, they are not "moons".

First Flights: The Montgolfier Brothers

When the Wright Brothers took off at Kittyhawk in 1903, people had already been flying for over a century. In fact, the first manned flights were launched in front of huge crowds in Paris, just a few years before the French Revolution. But they did not happen in airplanes.

For thousands of years, the Chinese had been making "Konming Lanterns". These were paper bags attached to a small wooden frame which held a candle. The warm air from the candle gathered in the bag, causing the lantern to float off into the sky. Although used primarily for religious festivals, they were also used on the battlefield as signalling devices. When a Brazilian priest living in Lisbon, Father Bartolomeu de Gusmão, used the heat from a candle to float a small paper bag at the court of King John V in 1709, he had probably gotten the idea from descriptions given to him by fellow Portuguese clergymen who had been to China.

The ancient Chinese did have the technological capability of constructing a larger version of the Konming Lantern—big enough to carry a human aloft—but there is no indication that they ever tried it. Renaissance Europe almost certainly knew of the Chinese lanterns, but never did anything with the idea.

In 1782, a pair of brothers in Paris, Jacques-Etienne and Joseph-Michael Montgolfier, began their own experiments. They owned a paper-making shop, and one day one of the brothers had happened to see a paper bag, filled with hot air from the machinery, float off the floor. With bigger bags, they found that they could lift objects into the air—and the idea came that if they made their *balon* bag large enough, they could lift a person into the air. They could fly.

Using taffeta cloth that was glued over with strips of paper, the brothers had a material that was sufficiently light, strong and airtight to make large bags, which they heated up with a straw-fueled fire built underneath. Not realizing that it was the less-dense hot air that was producing the buoyancy needed for flight, the brothers thought they had found a new type of gas that was lighter than air, which they referred to, immodestly, as "Montgolfier Gas".

Confident in their new gadget, the Montgolfiers announced that they would make a public flight of their balloon on June 4, 1783. The 33-foot bag was inflated by hot air from a fire on the ground at the Anonnay Marketplace and was then released. Unmanned and unguided, the balloon rose steadily, climbing quickly to an estimated 5-6000 feet, and floated off on the wind. With no fire on board, the air inside the bag began to cool, causing the balloon to steadily descend. It stayed aloft for 10 minutes before settling back on the ground, covering a distance of over a mile.

The "hot-air balloon" had been born. But it already had competition.

In 1766, almost 20 years before the Montgolfier brothers thought they had discovered a new gas, the English chemist Henry Cavendish had in fact discovered the gaseous element hydrogen and studied its properties. One immediately obvious characteristic was that hydrogen gas was lighter than air, and floated upwards. Years later, an experimenter in Paris named Jacques-Alexandre Charles came upon Cavendish's work and immediately grasped what this meant: if he could fill a large gas-tight bag with hydrogen, it could produce enough lifting power to carry a human.

Making enough hydrogen gas for such a device was the easy part. By mixing iron and sulphuric acid, he produced a chemical reaction that released pure hydrogen gas. The hard part was constructing a large durable bag that was sufficiently gas-tight to be inflated. After a series of experiments, Charles found a workable method: he sewed pieces of silk to form a bag and coated this with a solution of rubber dissolved in turpentine, which sealed all the seams and prevented the hydrogen from passing through the cloth.

By August 1783, Charles was ready for a demonstration flight of his gas balloon. The bag he built was about 12 feet wide, and had lift sufficient to carry about 20 pounds. On August 27, after filling his *balon* with hydrogen gas in front of a large crowd of Parisians at the Champ du Mars, he released it. The American ambassador to France, Benjamin Franklin, was among the spectators who watched as the balloon lifted into the sky, reaching a height of several hundred feet and drifting northwards with the wind. As people on horseback followed along, it flew for 45 minutes before landing in the little village of Gonesse. The experiment then ended ignominiously, as the terrified peasants of Gonesse, thinking that any large thing that had drifted silently down from the sky must be demonic, attacked the balloon and tore it apart with their pitchforks.

The next logical step was a manned flight, and both Charles and the Montgolfiers made their plans. The brothers were ready first. Louis XVI, the King of France, had heard about the earlier flights and was interested, and invited them to make their next flight from the grounds at the Royal Palace. Their new balloon, made with the help of local wallpaper manufacturer Jean-Baptiste Reveillon, was 30 feet in diameter and was decorated with zodiacal signs and suns, in honor of the French "Sun Kings".

Since nobody knew anything at all about how the human body would react to the cold thin air at high altitudes, it was decided that a test flight would be made first. King Louis helpfully offered to provide a couple of condemned criminals as test subjects to be sent aloft, but the Montgolfier brothers decided on a more scientific selection of pasengers: they would send a sheep, a duck, and a rooster. The sheep, they concluded, was a good stand-in for a human, being about the same in size and lung capacity. The duck and rooster would be the "controls" in the experiment; since ducks often fly at high altitude it was expected that the balloon ride would not effect it at all, and the rooster, being a bird that did not fly to high altitudes, provided an additional check on the flight's effects. To hold the passengers, a woven wicker basket was attached at the bottom, hanging below the balloon.

All was ready within a month, and on September 19, 1783, the first air passengers lifted off. Eight minutes later, they were back on the ground, and all were happy and healthy. It was the human's turn now.

Once again, the Montgolfiers politely turned down Louis's offer of some prisoners as human guinea pigs, and instead selected a Paris professor named Jean-François Pilâtre de Rozier and a French military officer named Francois Laurent Marquis d'Arlanders as the first air travelers. The balloon, now named the *Aerostat Reveillon,* was modified: the bag was almost 50 feet wide, and the wicker basket was replaced with a circular wooden platform where the passengers stood. To give a longer flight, they would carry a fire along with them in an iron tray slung in the center of the platform. The balloon bag was fireproofed by coating it with alum. In October a final test was made by raising the tethered balloon to a height of several hundred feet with Pilâtre de

Rozier aboard, and when he showed no ill effects from the altitude, the flight was ready.

On November 21, 1783, the *Aerostat Reveillon* lifted off from the Bois de Boulogne, in front of a cheering crowd that included King Louis XVI, his wife Queen Marie Antoinette, and US ambassador Benjamin Franklin. Franklin later wrote, "We observed it lift off in the most majestic manner. When it reached around 250 feet in altitude, the intrepid voyagers lowered their hats to salute the spectators. We could not help feeling a certain mixture of awe and admiration." Reaching an altitude of around 500 feet, the balloon covered a little over five miles in 25 minutes. The fire had enough straw fuel aboard for at least another hour; however the pair became concerned when sparks began smoldering on the alum-coated paper envelope, and decided to land. But for the first time in history, humans had flown. The "Montgolfier Balloon" became a sensation. In one of the first examples of "merchandising", commemorative dinnerware was produced with depictions of the flight; clocks were made in the shape of a balloon. The brothers became the most famous people in Paris. By January 1784, just two months later, larger versions of their hot-air balloon were carrying groups of up to seven people and reaching altitudes over 3000 feet.

But the future of flight did not belong to them. When Jacques-Alexandre Charles finally got his new hydrogen gas balloon ready on December 1, 1783, ten days after the Montgolfier balloon's flight, he conclusively demonstrated that his was the superior flying apparatus. The hydrogen balloon did not need a fire or fuel, its gas bag could carry it higher and further, and with sandbags as ballast it could be raised and lowered at will. The first manned flight of a hydrogen balloon took off from the Royal Garden at the Tuileries in front of a crowd of 400,000 Parisians, including the King, Queen, much of the French nobility, and, once again, Benjamin Franklin. Also on hand to watch was Joseph-Michael Montgolfier. It was piloted by Charles and one of his partners, Nicolas-Louis Robert. The gas balloon reached an altitude of 1800 feet (Charles was carrying a barometer and a thermometer with him to take measurements), and flew over two hours before setting down at dusk, 25 miles away.

About a year later, in January 1785, the first successful balloon flight was made across the English Channel. It was a hydrogen gas balloon. When lightweight gasoline engines became available in the 1890's, steerable "airships", which used hydrogen bags for lift and engine-driven propellers for steering, began to appear. Airships were used for a variety of civilian and military uses until the 1930s, when airplanes became cheaper, faster and safer.

Nakhimov: The Ship That Sunk Twice

In August 1986, the Soviet cruise liner Admiral Nakhimov *collided with a freighter while leaving port and was sunk, killing over 400 people. It was the worst shipping disaster in Soviet history. And strangely enough, this was not the first time the ship had been sunk.*

Before the age of jet air travel, the only method of crossing the Atlantic between the United States and Europe was by passenger liner. Although the trans-Atlantic traffic was dominated by British ships like the *Olympic* and the *Mauretania,* the Germans also had a significant share of the market. One of the German passenger liners that served the Atlantic routes was the *Berlin,* constructed in 1925 in the Vegesack Shipyard by the North German Lloyd shipping line. The third German liner to bear the name, the *Berlin* measured 572 feet long, and carried about 1000 passengers per trip between New York and Bremen. From 1925 to 1938, she criss-crossed the North Atlantic, her routine service only interrupted once, in November 1928, when the liner *Vestris* was sunk in a storm off the coast of Virginia, and the nearby *Berlin* was dispatched to the scene to help pick up survivors.

In 1938, the Hitler regime introduced a program that they called "Strength Through Joy", a morale-building exercise which took groups of ordinary German workers on luxury cruises. As part of this program, the German government confiscated the *Berlin,* using her for a number of cruises before, on the eve of World War II, converting her to a hospital ship. From 1940 to 1944, "*Hospital Ship A*" ferried wounded troops from the battlefield to medical facilities in Germany and Norway.

By the end of 1944, the Soviet Army was pushing the Nazis into a full retreat, and the Germans began a massive effort to transport wounded German soldiers as well as civilian refugees out of Eastern Europe. Several former passenger liners were pressed into this service, and one of them was the *Berlin.* On January 31, 1945, while forming up as part of a convoy, the *Berlin* hit a floating Russian mine and was severely damaged. Taken in tow by another ship, she was on her way to the port of Kiel for repairs when, around midnight, she hit another mine. This time the damage was too extensive, and the *Berlin* began sinking. But because she was in shallow water at the time, she settled on the bottom with about half her height still above water. Nearly all of the crew and passengers got off safely. For the next five years she stayed there as an abandoned derelict, half-submerged.

After the war ended, the area where the *Berlin* lay rusting was now a part of Poland, in the Soviet orbit. The USSR had suffered enormous economic devastation from the war, and the Russians were keen to salvage anything that was useful, particularly if it had formerly belonged to Germany. The wreck of the *Berlin* caught their attention. Seizing her as "war reparations", the Soviets launched an amazing effort to patch up all the damage in the ship's hull, pump out all the water to re-float her, then replace most of the interior (increasing her displacement by about 2000 tons). In 1949, the resurrected *Berlin* now joined the Russian fleet as an un-named transport vessel for the Soviet Foreign Ministry.

In 1957, the ship was once again re-fitted, this time as a passenger cruise ship. Now named the *Admiral Nakhimov,* after a hero of the Crimean War, she was assigned to the Black Sea Shipping Company (BLASCO) and was based in the resort city of Odessa, where she began regular cruises to ports in Turkey. During the Missile Crisis in October 1962, the *Nakhimov* was temporarily diverted for use as a troop transport, delivering a number of Soviet soldiers and military technicians to Cuba. She then returned to civilian service, adding occasional cruises to Havana on her schedule.

Although she was still being promoted as "the pride of the Black Sea", by 1986 the *Nakhimov* was showing her age and had been eclipsed by newer and more modern ships. She was already in the process of being scheduled for decommissioning and scrapping.

On the night of August 31, 1986, the *Nakhimov* was partway through her routine six-day cruise around the Black Sea to Turkey, and had just left the port at Novorossysk en route to the resort city of Sochi. On board were 888 passengers and 346 crew. At 10:30pm, just as the ship was approaching the mouth of the harbor, Captain Vadim Markov noticed a blip on his radar. It was the Soviet freighter *Pyotr Vasev,* returning from Canada with a load of grain. The night was so clear that Markov could see the *Vasev's* lights on the horizon. According to the maritime rules of traffic, the incoming *Pyotr Vasev* had the right of way, but Captain Markov radioed the approaching freighter and asked it to give way to the *Nakhimov,* so his passengers would not be delayed. The freighter's captain, Victor Tkachenko, replied that it would be alright—they had plenty of room to pass. Thus satisfied, Captain Markov turned over command of the *Nakhimov* to his first officer, Alexander Chudnovsky, and went to bed.

But something was going wrong. Shortly before 11pm, Chudnovsky noticed that the *Pyotr Vasev* had not altered its course or speed, and was getting close to the *Nakhimov*. Contacting the *Vasev* by radio, he was again assured that there would be "no problem". But still there was no change in the freighter's course or speed. As the incoming ship loomed closer and closer, her lights ablaze, Chudnovsky now altered his own course by ten degrees, then a few minutes later turned another ten degrees. But the *Vasev* continued to approach, and at ten minutes after 11 it was apparent that there would be a collision. Chudnovsky ordered a sharp turn to try and get out of the way, and on board the *Pyotr Vasev*, Captain Tkachenko now ordered his engines put to full astern to try to stop, but it was already too late. Each ship weighed over 17000 tons, and their momentum inexorably brought them together. Up on deck, some of the *Nakhimov's* passengers were watching helplessly as the freighter bore down on them. Two minutes later came the impact.

The bow of the freighter punctured the hull of the passenger ship squarely in the boiler room, penetrating at least 20 feet. The *Nakhimov's* forward momentum dragged the *Vasev's* bow back along her hull, ripping open an immense hole some 30 by 30 feet and exposing several decks to the ocean. The waters of the Black Sea began pouring in at a rate of tons per second. The liner took an immediate list to starboard, and as the *Nakhimov* leaned over, the portholes were submerged. Because the ship's antiquated ventilation system did not work very well, nearly every porthole on the ship was open, and now this added to the water flooding into the hull.

Of the several hundred passengers who had already retired to their cabins for the night, virtually none survived. The impact had torn up the ship's generators and shut off the electricity, including the lights, and as the *Nakhimov* continued to lean over sideways, it was impossible for passengers to find their way out. The huge tear in the hull and the open portholes allowed so much water to enter that after just four minutes the ship was laying on its side, and only four minutes later the *Admiral*

Nakhimov had disappeared under 150 feet of water. There had not been time to launch even a single lifeboat.

Fortunately, however, most of the *Nakhimov's* passengers had been on the upper deck, either at a dance party or watching a movie in one of the ship's theaters. The *Pyotr Vasev,* which had backed away a short distance after the collision, began picking survivors out of the water almost immediately, and other rescue ships arrived within ten minutes. Of the 1,234 crew and passengers on the *Nakhimov,* 423 were drowned.

The secretive Soviet Union did not like reporting on things that had gone wrong, and news of the disaster was not officially released until two days later. A government inquiry was launched under the Maritime Ministry, which concluded that both Captain Markov of the *Admiral Nakhimov* and Captain Tkachenko of the *Pyotr Vasev* had been criminally negligent in their duty. Both men were sentenced to 15 years in prison, but both were released in 1992, after the collapse of the USSR. Neither has spoken about the incident since, and there is still no clear understanding of how the two ships collided despite being in visual and radio contact with each other.

The House of Hanover: How a Minor German Noble Became the King of England

Nothing symbolizes "England" more than the Royal family, the House of Windsor. But in reality, the Windsor family is not English at all—it is German. How a German aristocrat came to be King of England and form a dynasty that would rule for 300 years (most recently under an assumed name), is a story of religious conflict and near-civil war.

In 1688, as the "Glorious Revolution" came to an end, King James II of England fled the country. For centuries, since the time of the Reformation, Catholics and Protestants had been fighting each other all across Europe, as conflict over religious ideology merged with political conflict over the so-called "divine right of kings". In the Catholic countries, it was assumed that the King was King because God wanted him to be King, and, with the blessing of the Pope, the Monarch held absolute power. In the Protestant countries, by contrast, the authority of the Pope was rejected, and the "divine power" of the Monarch was checked by a Parliament, a legislature made up of lower nobles.

Although he ruled a country that was nearly all Protestant, King James II of England had been Catholic, and firmly embraced the ideology of "divine right". That inevitably led to conflict with Parliament and unpopularity with the public—a conflict which King James lost. After King James' departure, Parliament declared that his daughter Mary Stuart, a Protestant, would take his place as Monarch. She agreed only on the condition that her Dutch-born Protestant husband, William of Orange, be accepted as co-sovereign. Shortly after, in 1689, Parliament passed a Bill of Rights that weakened the power of the King and legally established the Parliament-appointed Ministers as the real holders of political power.

Queen Mary II and King William III had a short reign, however. Queen Mary died of smallpox in 1694, and William III died in 1700. That left Mary's sister Anne as Queen.

But Queen Anne's succession to the throne presented a potential political crisis. Although Anne had given birth to 17 children, all but one of them died in early childhood—and the survivor, the Duke of Gloucester, soon died at age 11. That left Queen Anne as the last of her Stuart line, without a direct heir. Further, an underground political movement had appeared, known as the "Jacobites", who were agitating for the return of the Catholic eldest son of James II, James Francis Stuart, as King James III. It was a potentially explosive situation.

To solve it, Parliament in 1701 passed the Act of Settlement, laying out new rules as to who could or could not be the English Monarch. The most important provision was that the Monarch could not be a Catholic or married to one, and had to swear a holy oath to uphold the Church of England under the title "Defender of the Faith".

Therefore, when Queen Anne died in 1714 without a direct heir, the Act of Settlement ruled out nearly all of the remaining Stuarts (who were Catholic), finally settling on George, a relatively minor nobleman of Brunswick-Luneberg, in the Hanover area of Germany. He was the son of Princess Sophia, who was herself the grand-daughter of England's King James I. George Hanover, who was 52nd in line to the English throne, became King George I of England. Not only had he never visited the British Isles, but he did not even speak a word of English.

With George I, the Stuart Dynasty came to an end, and the Hanover Dynasty began. It turned out to be a golden age for Britain. Over the next 100 years, under the Hanover Kings, England became the dominant world superpower, with an empire that stretched literally around the world (despite the loss of the American colonies under King George III). The era also saw the institutionalization of the current Constitutional Monarchy, with the Sovereign as symbolic head of state but real power in an elected Parliament. By the time Queen Victoria assumed the throne in 1837, the British Empire was the largest and richest society that had ever existed.

Queen Victoria, who was the grand-daughter of King George III, arranged marriages of her children and grand-children to most of the royal houses of Europe. As a result, when World War One broke out in August 1914, it pitted Kaiser Wilhelm II, Queen Victoria's grandson, against Tsar Nicholas II of Russia and King George V of England, also Victoria's grandsons. The three were cousins. Victoria's husband had been Prince Albert, of the German House of Saxe-Coburg-Gotha, and therefore King George V was also a member of that House. But in the anti-German hysteria that consumed England during the war, the name became something of an embarrassment. And so in 1917, at the height of the war, King George V first declared that his family was renouncing all of the hereditary titles that they held in Germany, and then shortly later announced that the family would be immediately changing its name and would no longer be the House of Saxe-Coburg-Gotha: "Now, therefore, We, out of Our Royal Will and Authority, do hereby declare and announce that as from the date of this Our Royal Proclamation Our House and Family shall be styled and known as the House and Family of Windsor, and that all the descendants in the male line of Our said Grandmother Queen Victoria who are subjects of these Realms, other than female descendants who may marry or may have married, shall bear the said Name of Windsor." When Kaiser Wilhelm heard the news, he is said to have joked that he was going to see the Shakespeare play "The Merry Wives of Saxe-Coburg-Gotha".

The Act of Settlement of 1701 was in legal force in England for over 300 years. As recently as 1998, the Earl of St Andrews was removed from the line of succession to the British throne after he married a Catholic. Then, in 2013, a new Act of Succession to the Crown was passed, which ended the anti-Catholic requirement.

The Slate Belt

Northeast Pennsylvania is most famous for its once-thriving coal mining industry. But centered near the same area was another mining trade that was just as important in the late 19th century—and became known as the Slate Belt.

Since medieval times, slate has been highly-valued as roofing material. Slate is formed, geologically, from compressed mud and shale, and its layered structure means that it can be split along the bedding planes to form flat thin sheets, perfect for roof shingles. Unlike wooden shingles, slate does not rot or warp, is fireproof, and is durable enough to withstand the elements for decades. It was the preferred material for estate manor houses and churches. However, because slate was relatively rare in Europe and required large amounts of labor to extract and prepare, it was reserved for only the most expensive of buildings.

When English colonists settled in Pennsylvania, though, they found large deposits of slate. These were often taken advantage of to provide roofing shingles for farmhouses and barns. Over time, new uses were found for the stone, and it became an important industrial material. Schoolhouse blackboards and writing slates, billiard table tops, kitchen counters, grave markers, and, in later years, telephone exchange boards, were all made from slate. But by far the most extensive use was for roofing, and soon slate from Pennsylvania was being shipped all over the country.

The largest deposits of high-quality slate were found in the "Blue Mountains" of upper Northampton County, between the Delaware and Lehigh Rivers just south of the Pennsylvania coal mining district. In 1848, a Welsh immigrant named Robert Jones, who had owned slate mines in Wales, settled in the Blue Mountains and founded the town of Bangor. Miners from Cornwall, in England, moved in shortly later, founding the towns of Wind Gap and Pen Argyl. The area around the three towns became known as "the Slate Belt".

Although there were soon dozens of small slate quarries in the area, Jones was the first "slater" to utilize industrial methods of mining. Where previously the slate had been dug out by hand, Jones introduced the use of dynamite to blast out large portions at a time. In later years, dynamite was replaced by precision drilling, which laid out a series of holes which could then be split to form uniform pieces. Chunks of rock weighing several tons were lifted out of the quarry with chain hoists, then tested for their suitability. The high-quality slate that separated cleanly into thin uniform layers, was set aside for splitting and shaping into shingles. The lower-quality rock went towards blackboards and other products. Some two-thirds of the tonnage that was quarried was flawed, either by cracks in the rock or by veins of other minerals, and these were discarded in huge waste piles, each over 100 feet tall. By the time Jones left Bangor to enlist in the Union Army in the Civil War, the Slate Belt, just 24 square miles, was producing over half of all the slate used in the United States

In the coal-mining regions just north of the Slate Belt, a network of railroads appeared to transport the coal, and the railroad companies themselves began buying up the coal mines and consolidating them. In the slate mines, however, there was virtually no rail transportation until 1879, when the Bangor-Portland Railroad was established. These trains were loaded with Portland cement manufactured in Nazareth and Martins Creek, then went the 15 miles north to Bangor and Pen Argyl to pick up a further cargo of slate tiles, finally delivering it all to ships at Port Morris, New Jersey. The Bangor-Portland Railroad never had any interest in acquiring the slate mines or the cement factories. The result was that each of the several dozen slate quarries that operated at any given time were independent small companies which were never bought up and consolidated into large corporations like the coal mines were.

Quarrying and moving the heavy slabs of slate was hard and dangerous work. The delicate task of splitting the rock, by hand, into thin layers and shaping them into finished products, like shingles or pool tables, required even more training and skill. "Slaters" were some of the highest-paid workers in the country, and this attracted groups of immigrants who left Europe for a better life in America. The original Pennsylvania slate miners were Welsh and Cornish, and they had worked slate quarries or coal mines in England. The next wave of immigrants into the area were from rural Germany. They became known as "Pennsylvania Dutch" (a corruption of "*Deutsch*", or "German"), and in addition to working the slate quarries, large numbers of them settled the rural Lehigh Valley as farmers.

By the 1890s, a wave of Italian miners began showing up in the Slate Belt. Unlike the earlier Anglo-Saxons from England and Germany, the arrival of the Italians caused racial and ethnic strife. The Italians lived in their own little enclave between Bangor and Pen Argyl, in a town they called "Roseto". As more wealth was produced by the slate quarries, other ethnic groups began to arrive: Irish, Polish, and Jews from Eastern Europe and Russia. The white population of the Slate Belt, in turn, responded with virulent racism, anti-semitism, and anti-catholicism. By 1900, Bangor and Pen Argyl had one of the most active branches of the Ku Klux Klan in Pennsylvania, and the local high school sports teams kept the name "White

Knights" for several decades afterwards (until political pressure forced a change to "Green Knights").

But the glory days of the Slate Belt were already ending. In 1903 the quarries employed over 4,000 miners and produced 140 million square feet of slate. It was the highest point they would ever see. Some of the quarries were drying up, running into low-quality rock called "hard tack". Slate roofing shingles began to be replaced by asphalt shingles, which, though far less durable, were very much cheaper, lighter, and easier to install. Demand for slate dropped, and although a handful of mines were able to hang on until the 1920's, producing specialty items like billiard tables, mausoleum vaults, and non-conducting electrical switchboards, newer plastics and metals soon replaced the quarried stone.

Dozens of mining companies went out of business, and the wealthy Slate Belt residents that had made their fortunes from the stone now moved to Allentown or Philadelphia. By the time the Great Depression hit in 1929, virtually all the Slate Belt mines had closed, leaving behind nothing but huge rain-filled open-quarry pits and towering slag piles of waste slate.

England's Bloodiest Day: The Battle of the Somme

In the entire 15 years of the Afghan War and the Second Iraq War, the United States suffered 58,000 casualties, including 6,600 deaths. On July 1, 1916, the British Army lost more than that during the first ***day*** *of the Battle of the Somme, making it the single bloodiest day in British history.*

When the First World War broke out in August 1914, both sides expected it to be over quickly. Instead, the war bogged down into a stalemate, with both sides dug into massive systems of trenches that ran from the English Channel all the way across Europe to the Swiss border. A typical defensive line consisted of two or three parallel trenches, with dug-out shelters and machine-gun positions, protected by sandbag walls and heavy bands of barbed-wire entanglements. They were virtually impregnable.

After several attempts by the allied Entente forces of France and Britain failed to break through the German trenchlines, the British concluded that this would now be a war of attrition, in which the strategic aim would simply be to kill the enemy troops faster than they could kill yours, until his forces became so depleted that he could no longer continue the war. To increase their own forces, the British, who had begun the war with just a small "British Expeditionary Force", now made a frantic effort under Lord Kitchener to recruit volunteers. One of these programs was the so-called "Pal's Battalions", in which groups of friends or "pals" were recruited and trained together and then sent to France as a single unit. In London, all the workers from a particular factory, or all the members of a fraternal order, would sign up together; in rural England, all the young men from an entire village would join as a single "Pal's Battalion". By the end of 1915, the British Army had over a million freshly-trained volunteers. They became known as "Kitchener's Mob".

Plans were immediately made to use them. In December 1915, the British and French began preparations for a massive frontal assault, along 25 miles of German trenches. This would be centered near the village of Thiepval along the Somme River, where the British and French trenchlines met. Before the attack, massed artillery would unleash the heaviest bombardment that had ever been seen—almost two million shells would be fired over a period of eight full days. The artillery barrage would, it was expected, destroy the German trenches and barbed-wire barriers, eliminate their artillery and machine gun emplacements, and allow the Entente troops to simply walk across No Man's Land and occupy the abandoned German lines. The attack would be made jointly by both French and British units. Although one of the objectives was to capture a number of villages and observation points, the primary aim was simply to kill as many Germans as possible and deplete their reserves. The massive assault was planned for August 1, 1916.

But the Germans beat them to the punch. The German General von Falkenhayn had also decided on a war of attrition, and had also planned a massive attack that would kill the Entente forces at a higher rate than they could kill his. The place von Falkenhayn chose for his assault was the ancient fortress at Verdun. Although of only marginal strategic value, the Verdun fortress was of enormous symbolic patriotic significance to France, and the Germans knew that no matter how many soldiers the French lost defending Verdun, they would continue to pour more and more forces in to defend it. The sole intent of his attack, von Falkenhayn asserted, was to "bleed the French Army white".

The Battle of Verdun, launched in early 1916, went just as von Falkenhayn expected. The French rallied around the defense of the fortress, adopting the popular slogan "They shall not pass!" As French losses mounted, units were pulled out of other sectors of the front and pushed into the Verdun meatgrinder, only to also be chewed up. With the French Army approaching collapse, the Entente generals decided that something had to be done quickly to relieve the pressure, and the only option readily available was the planned attack at the Somme. This was now advanced by 30 days, to take place on July 1, and its purpose changed; it was now intended to force the Germans to pull their units out of Verdun and use them to defend the Somme front.

On Saturday, June 24, the preliminary artillery barrage began. Over 1,500 British guns poured shells onto the German trenches for the next eight days. The British had also dug a series of tunnels that extended under No Man's Land all the way to the German trenches. Here, they packed underground chambers full of dynamite. At 7:30am on July 1, 1916, the Battle of the Somme was begun when 17 of these "mines" were detonated. They were, up to that time, the largest man-made explosions in history; according to later stories, the sound of their concussion could be heard all the way across the English Channel in London. They blew enormous craters into the German trenches, that are still visible today.

As the mines went off, the British troops climbed ladders out of their trenches and emerged into No Man's Land. They were each laden with some 75 pounds of weapons and equipment, and were under strict orders to walk, not run, across the bombed-out terrain towards the German trenches, taking care to keep a tightly-maintained formation. The British presumed they would meet very little opposition, with the intense artillery barrage having destroyed the German trenches.

They were wrong. The British bombardment was not nearly as effective as they expected. The shells had been manufactured by inexperienced factory workers in England and the United States, and about 20% of them failed to detonate. Those that did explode, had little effect; most of them were shrapnel shells, which were not very useful against barbed wire. The German wire entanglements were still mostly intact. The German troops, meanwhile, had sheltered in their deep dug-outs during the bombardment, and when the barrage ended, they quickly moved back into their positions. When the British troops emerged from their trenches and began walking across No Man's Land, the Germans were ready for them. Machine-gun fire swept across the fields, mowing down English soldiers by the hundreds. As "Pal's Battalions" were wiped out by machine guns, English villages lost their entire male populations at one stroke. By the time the troops were pulled back, the British Army had suffered 58,000 casualties, including 20,000 deaths. It remains the single worst day in all of British military history.

The French, meanwhile, had also attacked. The original plan was for about half the advancing troops to be French, but the disaster at Verdun had reduced their strength to only 20% of the Somme force. Unlike the British, however, who were going into battle for the first time, the French had already learned some hard lessons about trench warfare from their bitter experience at Verdun (which they had unsuccessfully tried to communicate to their British allies). While the British had in effect simply given advance warning to the Germans of the attack with their long but ineffective preliminary bombardment, the French had limited their "softening-up" barrage to just a few hours before the assault, thereby preserving some element of surprise. The French also reduced their casualties by advancing in small groups and moving from cover to cover, unlike the British who advanced in full line abreast at a walking pace. As a result, the French forces at the Somme, though smaller, were more successful—they captured several of their objectives and also suffered far fewer casualties.

But the Battle of the Somme did not end that day—or even that month. It would drag on, through assault after counter-assault, for the next five months, as both sides, each convinced that the other was about to collapse, continued to make "one more effort". The slaughter finally came to an end as winter set in, in November 1916. In the end, the battle had cost the British some 425,000 casualties and the French about 200,000; the Germans had lost about 500,000 men killed, wounded, and captured. In exchange, the Entente had advanced an average of just ten miles.

Although the initial press reports were censored, the massive casualties from the Somme could not be hidden, as entire neighborhoods got the telegrams at the same time. Even today, every rural English village has its church cemetery with a section where every grave bears the date "1916". The effect on morale was horrifying, and the British Army promptly stopped deploying men in "Pal's Battalions". The Battle of the Somme, more than any other battle of the war, came to symbolize the First World War in all its blood and mud and futility, and produced the image of the Entente armies that still prevails today—they were "lions, led by donkeys".

GI Joe vs the Volcano

In December 1935, the US Army Air Corps carried out the most unusual bombing mission of its entire history. This was no training flight—the pilots were carrying and delivering live bombs. But the target was not an enemy army, airfield, or fleet. The target was a volcano.

The "Big Island" of Hawaii is home to several active volcanoes, including Kilauea, Muana Loa, and Hualalai. These have been erupting for thousands of years, causing extensive lava flows, and were, according to the legends of the Hawaiian natives, the home of Pele, the flame-haired goddess.

In September and October 1935, a series of earthquakes shook the island. This was usually an indication that an eruption was imminent, as underground masses of molten rock pushed upward towards the surface. Dr Thomas Jaggar, director of the Hawaii Volcano Observatory, began to keep a close watch. On the morning of November 21, there was another large earthquake, and that afternoon red-hot lava began seeping out of cracks on Mauna Loa. The eruption had begun.

Hawaiian lava, because of its chemistry, tends to be fluid and thin; it flows easily and quickly, but also tends to cool rapidly. But as the lava flow cools on the outside, it forms a series of hollow "lava tubes" that can then insulate the molten rock inside from the air, allowing it to travel further. Much of the area around Mauna Loa was criss-crossed by these hollow lava tubes.

The 1935 eruption was rather placid until November 27, when a new volcanic vent opened on the north side of Mauna Loa. The new lava flow gathered into a natural bowl-shaped depression caused by earlier eruptions, where it formed a pool of molten rock. As more and more lava continued to flow, the level of this "lake of fire" continued to rise, until finally, on December 22, the lava overtopped the edges of the natural bowl which held it, and began flowing down the mountain again—directly towards the city of Hilo, some 20 miles away.

This presented a serious danger. Dr Jaggar's measurements indicated that the lava was advancing about 1.5 miles a day, channeling itself through the network of old lava tubes. At that rate, it would reach the city of 28,000 people by January 9, and destroy it completely.

Dr Jaggar had already been conducting a series of experiments to prepare for such an eventuality. Since the lava was being channeled through the lava tubes, he hypothesized that, using a series of carefully-placed dynamite explosions, he may be able to collapse particular tubes, dam the flow of lava within them until it cooled, and redirect the molten rock away from specific areas. Using mules to haul TNT up the mountain, he had already succesfully collapsed and sealed off old tubes with experimental explosions. Now, as Hilo was threatened by the lava heading its way, Dr Jaggar made plans to try out his method to divert the flow away from the city.

He quickly realized, though, that his plan would not work; he simply did not have enough time to gather a sufficient amount of explosives, carry them up the mountain by mule, place them all in specific spots, and detonate them. But then Guido Giacometti, his colleague at the Volcano Observatory came up with an alternative—perhaps the US Army Air Corps bombers, based over on Oahu at Pearl Harbor, would be able to do the job?

Dr Jaggar contacted the Army and explained his plan—by dropping aerial bombs on particular parts of the mountain, they might be able to divert the lava away from Hilo and save the city. The Army agreed to give it a try, and Lt Colonel George S Patton was placed in charge of the project. Patton assigned a flight of Keystone heavy bombers from the 23rd Bombardment Squadron and LB-6 light bombers from the 72nd Bombardment Squadron to the mission, and on the morning of December 26 they flew from their base at Luke Field to the auxilliary airfield at Hilo. One of the light bombers carried Dr Jaggar over Mauna Loa on a reconnaissance flight, allowing him to select specific targets. That evening, he briefed the bomber crews on his plan.

At 8:30am the next day, the bombers set out on their mission. The Keystones would be loaded with two 600-pound bombs each; the light bombers would trail behind as observers, including Dr Jaggar. They would return to Hilo, be refueled and reloaded, then go back to drop more bombs on the mountain.

While one bomb was a dud and failed to explode (it was found by National Park Service employees forty years later) most of the nineteen others were hits. Over the next few days, the flow of lava slowed, then stopped. Hilo had been saved. Dr Jaggar would later enthusiastically report, "The smashing of the tunnel had cooled the oncoming liquid so that it dammed itself. This confirmed the theory that the bombing solidified the tunnel lava back into the heart of the mountain....There can be no question whatever that the bombing stopped the flow." Newsreel footage at the time celebrated the Army flyers as heroes, and even today the insignia patch of the 23rd Bombardment Squadron depicts a rain of bombs falling on a volcano.

But given our current knowledge of vulcanology, it is pretty certain that Dr Jaggar's experiment actually did no good. His ideas were based on some assumptions about the chemistry of the rock that we now know are incorrect, and in any case the 600-pound bombs carried by the Air Corps were mere firecrackers compared to the flow of lava, and likely had no measurable effect on it. The lava had cooled and stopped all on its own.

But the US military never gave up on the idea. In early 1942, when Mauna Loa erupted again, the Air Corps sent a flight of B-18 bombers to drop some ordnance on the lava tubes, apparently without any noticeable effect. In 1974 the Air Force opined that perhaps what was needed were bigger bombs, so in 1975 and 1976, bombers dropped an experimental series of thirty-six 2,000 pound bombs on old lava tubes, to see what effect they could produce. Vulcanologists apparently pronounced the experiment a dud, and today nobody seriously proposes using explosions to put out volcanoes.

How "Traditional Chinese Medicine" Is Pushing Species to Extinction

Science shows that most of today's "traditional Chinese medicine" is simple quackery. But another consequence of the global "traditional medicine" industry that has not been as widely discussed is the enormous destructive effect it has had on some of the most endangered species on the planet.

For thousands of years, tribal humans used plants taken from nature as treatments and cures for diseases—because they had nothing else. By simple trial and error, some plants containing chemicals were indeed matched to diseases for which they were effective. The shamans and healers of course had no idea why or how these plants worked, so they attributed it to such things as "mystical energy" or "a gift of the gods".

Coming from pre-scientific religious and philosophical systems, however, most of these "traditional medicines" are based on nothing more than magic. Chinese "medicine" is based on the presumed flow through the body of the mystical energy "chi" which must be "balanced" through "yin" and "yang"—and illness is presumed to be the result of an "energy imbalance". Many traditional "cures" are based on "sympathetic magic"—the naive belief that a plant or animal's appearance or behavior tells of its medicinal properties. Tigers and bears for instance, were seen as powerful and virile animals, so it was presumed that eating tiger or bear parts would increase "male potency". (Recently, we have seen an example of this same magical thinking as it actually came into existence, when someone publicized the mistaken notion that sharks do not get cancer and the "alternative medicine" industry in turn suddenly began flooding us with dozens of "cures" and "preventatives" based on eating shark cartilage).

In Europe, the traditional view was that diseases were caused by an "imbalance" in the "four humours", and most "medicine" was aimed at reducing or increasing one of the "humours" to "restore the balance". After modern medical science demonstrated that the "four humours" framework was simply nonsense, the "traditional medicine" began to die out. As Europe and its colonies became wealthier and wealthier, doctors and hospitals replaced herbalists and shamans.

And, as nations like China and India undergo their own economic transformations, the same thing is happening today, as pre-scientific "cures" are being replaced by modern medicine which, unlike traditional religious magic, actually works, and which more and more people are now able to afford. But that societal transition is not an instant one. It takes a long period of time, during which a number of people still accept the traditional "cures", but now have the purchasing power to buy these things from anywhere on the planet. And, with their immense populations and steadily-increasing middle-class, the amount they can buy is enormous, and goes up every year. The effect has been devastating.

Animals

There are over 1500 different species of animal that are used in Indian and Chinese "traditional medicine". They range from turtles (which are supposed to promote longevity and also to increase the "yin" energy of the body and diminish the "yang") to monkey blood (which is supposed to cure all sorts of things, from achy joints to heart disease). The oddest (and sadly one of the most common) areas to be "cured" is male impotency. Among the "traditional medicine cures" proposed for this have been rhino horn, tiger penis, snake gall bladder, pangolin fetuses, sea horses, gecko lizards, cinnamon bark, and a few dozen others.

Since few of these animals can now be collected locally in India or China (partly because they have already been exterminated there by people using them for "traditional medicine"), they now have to be purchased overseas and imported. And as more and more of these rural poor are lifted out of poverty and raised to the middle class, they can afford to buy and import more and more of them. The legal trade of "medicinal" plants and animals imported into China alone is over $2 billion per year—and the illegal trade in smuggled plants and animals is much higher than that. But it is Mother Nature who pays the real price.

Rhinos

For half a century, rhinos have been the poster animals for endangered species. "Traditional medicine" has long held that powdered rhino horn is not only a cure for all sorts of various diseases and ailments, from fever to vomiting to headache to joint pain, but is also a powerful aphrodisiac that will cure male impotence. This is, of course, simply nonsense—rhino horn is made from compressed hair composed of the protein keratin, which is no different from your own hair or your fingernails. The association of "rhinos" with "male potency" comes solely because male rhinos have what are to human eyes absurdly big wee-wee's. (There's that "sympathetic magic" again.)

By the 1970s, all of the world's rhino species were on the verge of extinction, with poaching one of the primary causes. Some of this demand was centered in the oil-rich Middle East, where rhino horn was traditionally used for the handles of ceremonial daggers carried by desert tribesmen. But most poached rhino horn went to Asia for "medicine". Nations in eastern and southern Africa made tremendous efforts to combat poachers and protect their remaining rhino herds, with some measure of success. In some areas, the rhino populations began to slowly recover. But in the 1990's, rising wealth in China and

India began the process all over again. Poaching once more increased steadily, fueled by the growing demand for "medicinals" in Asia. Since the Asian species of rhino are now so critically rare that even the poachers have trouble finding them, most of the "traditional medicine" powdered horn in China comes from Africa. When a Vietnamese government official announced in 2006 that powdered rhino horn had cured his relative of cancer, there was an immediate spike in demand, an immediate increase in price—and over 300 White and Black Rhinos were poached in South Africa alone. Illegally-killed rhinos are now so insanely valuable on the black market that not even zoo rhinos are safe—zoos in Africa have had to hire armed guards to prevent poachers from entering at night and killing them. And with some two billion potential customers in China and India, there simply are not enough rhinos in the entire world to feed the demand.

Tigers

The Tiger is the most powerful and feared predator in all of Asia, so it is no wonder that it has been invested, in myth and folklore, with magical and semi-divine properties. And, also, in "traditional medicine". The "healing energy" of the Tiger, contained in its skin or its blood or its gall bladder or its powdered teeth/bones or its dried penis, is one of the most potent and highly-sought (and expensive) of all Indian and Chinese "traditional medicines"—touted as a cure for virtually everything and anything (including the old standby: wee-wee problems). In ancient days, of course, only the royals could afford to hunt tigers: today, any poor peasant with a hunting rifle can shoot a tiger and earn enough money to live on for several years. Tiger poaching became such a huge problem and provoked such international outrage that even China was forced to outlaw the import or sale of tiger products—though the law is seldom enforced (so much money flows into tiger-smuggling operations that bribery of police and local Communist Party government officials is just a routine business expense).

Pangolins

The Pangolin is an odd-looking mammal that was once found throughout southern Asia. Although it is a mammal, it does not have fur—instead it is covered by hard scales that make it look like a pine cone. These scales are actually flaps of compressed hair, and, like the rhino's horn, are composed mostly of the protein keratin. Pangolin scales have long been an ingredient in "traditional medicine", said to be a cure for such things as tumors and asthma. They are also considered to be a treatment for infertility and male impotence. For some reason that has been lost to history, some Taoist scholar long ago decided that the unborn fetus of the Pangolin was a particularly powerful "male enhancement".

Because Pangolins are solitary animals and do not have high population densities, they could once only be collected in relatively small numbers in the immediate locality. But today, modern technology has changed that. As China became more wealthy, and as more and more rich Chinese men decided that they needed a wee-wee treatment, the Pangolin became increasingly more targeted, and the price skyrocketed. In 1990, a kilogram of Pangolin scales would sell for about $14 (which was, at that time, quite a lot of money for a rural Chinese peasant). Today, the price has soared to $200, and Pangolin meat (especially the fetus) sells for over $1,000 per pound. As a result, the Chinese population of Pangolins was virtually wiped out, dropping from around 50,000 to less than 5,000. As the numbers decreased in China and the Pangolin became legally protected, poachers turned to the surrounding countries, and began wiping out their Pangolin populations too—first in India, Nepal and Pakistan, then in Southeast Asia, and now in Africa. In the two-year period from 2011 to 2013, at least 200,000 Pangolins were illegally smuggled into China, most of them passing through Indonesia or Vietnam. (And not just into China—from 2000-2009, 85 illegal shipments of Pangolin were seized as they attempted to enter the United States, intended for "traditional medicine" shops in big-city "Chinatowns".) As a result, the Pangolin is now considered to be "threatened" or "endangered" in nearly all of its global range.

Plants

To feed the enormous industry, many of the several thousand plants utilized in "traditional medicine" are now farm-raised, often on big plantations specially cleared for the purpose. But many other "medicinal" plants, for various reasons, cannot be grown commercially, and are therefore instead collected from the wild. And for many, the effects have been devastating. In 2008, the International Union for the Conservation of Nature (IUCN) and the wildlife monitoring group TRAFFIC did a joint study of just seven Asian plant species that were commonly used in Chinese and Indian "traditional medicine", and found that all seven (Himalayan Yew, Snakeroot, Red Sanders, Kutki, Jatamansi, Elephant's Foot and Desert Cistanche) were, despite legal protections under the CITES treaty on threatened and endangered species, being heavily harvested and illegally imported into India and China, and were under severe threat in their natural ranges. That same year, the Botanic Gardens Conservation International group listed several hundred "medicinal plants" that were being endangered through overcollection for the international market, including Hoodia, Warburgia, and Jaborandi. And in 2009 "The Times of India" newspaper looked at the status of 359 native plants utilized in traditional Ayurvedic "medicine" and found that a startling 335 of them, or 93 percent, were threatened or endangered, most of them due to overcollection.

The Future

In the short-term future, the problem will almost inevitably get worse. Despite the enormous ecological devastation that China's use of "traditional medicines" has already caused, there are still over 800 million rural Chinese living in poverty, and as China's economy grows and they too are lifted into a middle-class lifestyle, they will add to the demand for wild plants and animals, more than doubling the damage China is doing. Most of India's population will also reach a similar economic level in just a few years. And waiting in the wings are other currently-poor nations with high populations who will in the near future undergo their own economic expansion—Indonesia, Vietnam, Cambodia—and add to the demand.

Ultimately, the only long-term solution to the problem that will actually work is education: people in poor rural countries will need to be taught that religious- and philosophy-based "medicine" doesn't actually cure anything, that drinking cobra blood will not treat your fever, that maple bark will not relieve your arthritis, and that eating Tiger or Pangolin will not make your wee-wee get hard. (And then those poor rural people will need to be provided with actual effective medical care that will help them.) Most of the affected governments acknowledge this pressing need, but also point out that even if they had the resources to carry out such a massive program (and most of them don't), the effort would still take years, perhaps decades. And for many of these wild animal and plant species, that will be way too late.

Drafting Dolphins: A History of the Military's Marine Mammal Program

During the Cold War, the US Navy trained dozens of dolphins and sea lions to perform military tasks, such as locating mines and detecting enemy special forces swimmers and divers.

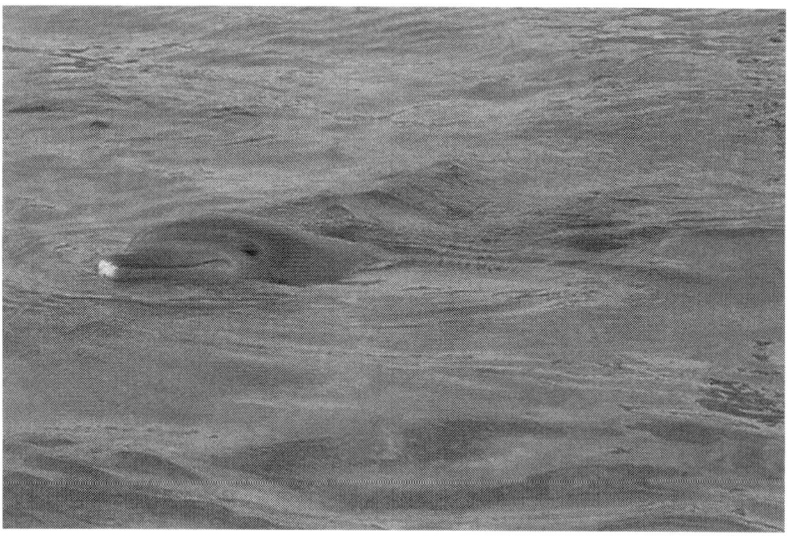

When it comes to water, we humans are virtually helpless. Even with all the benefits of modern diving technology, we are slow and ponderous underwater, we can't see very well, we can't go very deep and can only stay there for short periods (and must then spend a long time "decompressing"). Marine mammals like dolphins, orcas and sea lions, on the other hand, are perfectly adapted to life in the water—they can swim rapidly and can execute deft precise maneuvers at virtually any depth, they can see at least five times further underwater than we can, especially in low light, they have excellent hearing which is, in whales and dolphins, supplemented by sophisticated echolocation systems, and they are intelligent animals which are readily trainable. As always, Mother Nature is better than our best technology.

It is little wonder, then, that the military took a keen interest in these animals, and found ways to utilize their natural abilities. During the Cold War both the United States and the Soviet Union were training marine mammals to carry out military operations. Most of these programs are still heavily classified, but over the decades some details have leaked out, giving us some idea of what they do and how they do it.

The Navy's initial interest in dolphins was centered around submarines. The US was building and deploying nuclear-armed Polaris missile submarines, and thought that by studying dolphins, engineers could learn how to make their subs more streamlined, faster, and quieter. In 1959 a military team was sent to collect data from the dolphins at Marineland in California.

The idea for more direct uses began in 1964, when sonar expert Dr James Fitzgerald casually remarked to some Navy brass at a party in Annapolis that dolphins, with their sophisticated sonar systems, might be useful to the military. At this time, most people knew "dolphins" only from the TV show "Flipper" and from performing shows at tourist aquariums. The Navy liked the idea, and soon captured a number of wild Pacific White-Sided Dolphins and Atlantic Bottlenose Dolphins (in later years the Navy started captive-breeding its own marine mammals) and began training them. Most of the training happened in California, while cold-water operations were conducted in Alaska.

Training a dolphin isn't much different than training a dog. The most effective process is called "positive reinforcement". The desired actions are broken down into a series of simple steps which are then taught individually and later strung together. When the trainee animal performs the desired action, it is rewarded with a food treat or with lavish social attention. And when the trainee fails to perform the requested action, there is no coercion or punishment—instead the animal is simply ignored. Over time, the animal learns to perform on request a number of complex tasks. A typical dolphin would spend five or six years in training, and individual dolphins were specialized in different military programs. Over the years more species of marine mammal such as California sea lions, orcas (or "killer whales"), belugas, and pilot whales, which could dive deeper, swim further, were more maneuverable, or were physically stronger than dolphins, were added to the training. The program became known as the Marine Mammal System (MMS), which was later expanded into the Advanced Marine Biological Systems (AMBS) and then renamed the Navy Marine Mammal Program (NMMP).

The first known use of a military-trained dolphin was in 1965. As part of its SEALAB project to carry out longterm underwater research, the US Navy had a number of divers living for weeks at a time in an ocean-floor module off the coast of California. One of the dolphin trainees, named Tuffy, was taught to deliver mail to the underwater "aquanauts".

But when the US began its involvement in Vietnam, the Navy's ambitions expanded rapidly. Various groups of dolphins were separated into different projects, each with its own particular military task. We only know about a few of them. The project known as MK4 trained dolphins to find naval anti-ship mines that were tethered to the sea floor, and mark them with an electronic locator or floating buoy for later destruction. Project MK5 taught California sea lions to find various sorts of objects on the seafloor—things like torpedos, mines, and bombs, and, some rumors say, lost nuclear weapons—and attach "grabber" devices with cables so they could be recovered. The techniques worked equally well for accidentally-lost American weapons and for Soviet weapons that the US wished to examine, especially in very deep water where human divers could not go. MK6 trained dolphins and sea lions to serve as underwater sentries around ports or ships, to swim around and find enemy swimmers or special-forces teams (and, perhaps, kill them). The MK7 program used dolphins to find lost objects on the sea floor, but took advantage of their sonar to also locate objects that were buried in the sediment. Project MK8 used teams of dolphins to find and mark underwater mines or anti-ship obstacles at potential Marine landing beaches. The Navy has not acknowledged that dolphins were also trained to attach explosive limpet mines to the underwater hulls of enemy ships, which would then be remotely detonated to sink them, but we know from leaked information that they were. They also were apparently trained to attach electronic trackers or listening devices to the hulls of enemy ships and submarines. It is likely that all of these programs, plus new ones that we don't know about, are still in service today.

Much of what the AMBS-trained dolphins did in Vietnam remains classified. Ironically, most of what we know comes from the archives of the former Soviet Union, who were backing their North Vietnamese allies. From the reports of Russian Spetsnaz "special forces" teams who were operating in Vietnam, we know that the US had deployed dolphins from the MK6 project to patrol places like ports and Navy bases. The Soviets recorded that two of their Spetsnaz divers, who were planting a limpet mine on an American cargo ship, had been killed by American dolphins, and as a result the Russians began training their special forces to defend themselves against the animals—and also began a marine mammal program of their own. We do not know exactly how the American dolphins killed the swimmers, but leaked information in the 1970's revealed that both sea lions and dolphins had been trained in anti-personnel attacks. The animals had been taught to approach enemy divers and tear off their air hose and face mask, forcing them to the surface and exposing them to "other security assets". The highly-maneuverable sea lions were also trained to attach a special clamp to a diver's leg. This prevented him from swimming and also contained an electronic marking device, allowing US divers to locate him. Some of the clamps would reel out a thin but strong line which the sea lion carried to a nearby US patrol boat, allowing them to literally pull the enemy diver in like a fish. And, according to some leaked sources, some of the dolphins carried a special gas gun, originally designed for divers as a defense against sharks, strapped to their nose. This was a long barbed hollow needle that was attached to a canister of compressed CO2 gas, which could be triggered either on impact or remotely to inject the gas into the diver, which then explosively expanded inside him and produced what was presumably a messy death.

At its peak, during the Reagan years, the marine mammal program had over 100 dolphins, an unknown number of other animals, and a budget of $8 million. Congress granted a partial exemption to the Marine Mammal Protection Act which allowed the Pentagon to take a number of dolphins and whales from the wild for "national defense purposes". (Today, the Navy says, it captive-breeds all its own animals, and begins training them within several weeks of birth.) When the Cold War ended, the Navy reduced the program, gave away about one-third of its marine mammals, and declassified information about the existence of the program (but did not release any of the operational details.)

The existence of the military dolphin program, however, had already been revealed through a leak in the 1970's, and it provoked a storm of outrage from environmentalists and animal-welfare activists. The Navy denied that it was mis-treating any of the animals (pointing out that it cost a lot of money to train each of them), and also denied that the animals were being used to actually kill people. When citizens sued the Navy in the 1980s over a plan to use dolphin and sea lion sentries in Puget Sound to guard the Trident Submarine Base there, the court appointed independent reviewers to examine the conditions under which they were being kept. They found that the Navy animals had a survival rate of over 95%, the highest of any organization worldwide that maintains large numbers of marine mammals.

The marine mammal program next appeared in action during the Second Gulf War, when, during the invasion of Iraq, six dolphins were used to clear beaches ahead of Marine landings, uncovering at least 100 anti-ship mines. Other dolphins were used to search captured Iraqi ports for mines, and trained Sea Lions were deployed in harbors where US ships were anchored, to patrol for enemy swimmers and saboteurs. This program was known as the Shallow Water Intruder Detection System (SWIDS). Similar programs had been used in the 1980s during American interventions in the Middle East, and during the Iran-Iraq War the dolphins had been used to search for mines inside Persian Gulf shipping lanes.

In all, the Navy acknowledges having deployed trained marine mammals in 25 countries (and though we don't know all of the countries, we do know that the list includes Vietnam, Iraq, Bahrain, and South Korea). One of those nations was the US itself, where dolphin sentries have been used to patrol many Navy ports and submarine bases. In 1996, trained dolphins and sea lions were sent to patrol San Francisco Bay, to help protect the Republican Party National Convention. Today, the US program consists of 80 dolphins and 30 sea lions. The Soviet Union also had an active marine-mammal program, which continued in Russia after the end of the Cold War. According to documents, the USSR trained some of its dolphins as living torpedos, strapping an explosive charge to them and sending them to swim underneath an enemy ship. The Russians also rather cleverly designed a parachute harness for their dolphins, which allowed them to be dropped from an airplane: the US in turn developed a small boat with a hatch in the hull for the clandestine release of dolphins and sea lions.

As of 2016, there are reports that the marine mammal program may be in the process of being phased out. Modern electronic underwater drones have become so sophisticated that they can now perform most of the tasks that the dolphins and sea lions were trained for. So it is possible that the Navy's 110 dolphin and sea lion warriors may soon be unemployed, perhaps to end their days entertaining children in a zoo or marine park.

The Strange Case of the Cyanide Grass

In 2012, a pasture full of cows were killed by cyanide poison. But this was not the result of a malicious human act—the poison came from the grass they were eating. And the "killer cyanide grass" became an Internet sensation.

In June 2012, a Texas cattle rancher named Jerry Abel released a herd of 18 cattle onto a patch of pasture. At first, nothing seemed out of the ordinary. Then, the cows started bellowing, staggering around, and falling to the ground, convulsing. Within minutes, fifteen of them were dead. Necropsies on the dead cows revealed something startling and completely unexpected—they had all died from cyanide poisoning. But where had the poison come from?

It has long been known that many varieties of plants produce toxins as a method of protecting themselves from herbivores. Since plants cannot run away from animals that want to eat them, they must resort to chemical warfare, and manufacture an enormous variety of compounds in their tissues that discourage herbivores (especially insects) from chewing on them. These include chemicals that are extracted and used in some of our most common foods and medicines: peppermint, spearmint, digitalis, aspirin, caffeine, opiates, nicotine, vanilla—all of these are basically insecticides, designed to sicken or kill bugs that try to eat the plant's leaves, stems, or seeds. For larger herbivores such as deer or cattle or goats, the plants have more potent chemical weapons—such as urushiol (the irritant found in poison ivy), or oxalic acid.

One very common plant weapon is hydrogen cyanide. This is found most often in the sorghum family of plants, but is also common in other groups. The cyanide is manufactured and stored in the plant's cells, where it is connected to a sugar molecule that makes it inert. When eaten, the sugar molecule is broken, releasing the poison. In most instances, the amount of toxin that is released is just enough to sicken the animal and make it stop eating the plants, but it is not unknown for animals (and humans) to sometimes get a fatal dose. Among the everyday plants that store cyanide precursors are wheat, barley, oats, rye, French beans, kidney beans, lima beans, apples, peaches, plums, apricots, cherries, almonds, Macadamia nuts, quince, papaya, passion fruit, bamboo shoots, cassava root, and taro root. And grass.

Once it was determined that the cows in Texas had been killed by cyanide, attention immediately turned to the grass they had been eating. Rancher Abel's pasture had been planted with a variety of grass seed known as Tifton-85. This is a variety of bermuda grass that was bred by researchers at the University of Georgia in 1990. Like virtually all agricultural plants, Tifton-85 is a hybrid. Hybridization, used for hundreds of years to produce new varieties of all sorts of plants, from roses to wheat, is simple "cross-breeding", in which two varieties of plant are bred together to move desirable characteristics from one breed to the other. In the case of Tifton-85, it was intended to produce a high-protein grass for use in cattle pastures that could withstand the heat and humidity of the southeastern United States. University researchers took an existing bermuda grass and crossed it with a closely-related variety of star grass. The resulting hybrid produced more grass per acre, had deeper root systems, and was more tolerant of southern climates. It became commercially available in the 1990s: Jerry Abel had been using it on his ranch for 15 years.

As it happens, several varieties of grass, including bermuda grass, star grass, sudan grass, rye grass and crab grass, naturally produce cyanide precursors in their tissues as defenses against herbivores. Under normal conditions, the amount is small and the dosage of cyanide is so tiny that it is harmless (just like in the almonds that we eat). However, it has long been known that when the plants suffer environmental stress, they sometimes respond by increasing their production of poison precursors. And when the grasses in Jerry Abel's ranch were examined, they turned out to have elevated levels of cyanide—as did other ranches in the area. Texas had, for the past two years, been undergoing a serious drought. It was concluded that the grasses, under the prolonged stress, had responded by manufacturing unusually high levels of cyanide precursors in their tissues, and when the cows ate the grass they unknowingly released the fatal toxin.

The dangers presented by potentially toxic cyanide in pasture grasses and other plants had long been known and discussed in both the scientific literature and in animal-management texts, and incidents like that at Jerry Abel's ranch had already happened before. But Abel's cows had dropped dead in the Age of the Internet, and as a result they became the center of a media sensation that still echoes years later.

On the day the cows died, a local CBS affiliate picked up the story and ran it on its website. Unfortunately, the initial story contained information that was simply not true. The Tifton-85 hybrid was erroneously identified as a "genetically-modified organism" or GMO. Since GMOs are the subject of much fear and hysteria amongst a certain segment of people, websites all over the Internet began screaming the "Poisonous GMO Plants Kill Cows!" story, many of which added details that were simply wrong, such as that the cows had been killed by a cloud of "poison gas" released by the plants, and that humans were in potential danger from cyanide-releasing grasses on golf courses or lawns. None of this was accurate (there were no GMO varieties of grass—they were all simple hybrids, and the cyanide was only dangerous if the grass itself was eaten), and CBS ran an immediate correction, but the sensationalized stories about the "killer GMO grass" can still be found today on anti-science advocacy websites, passed around by people who did not bother to do any fact-checking.

The real lesson of the Texas cow massacre is a simple one that we often tend to forget: in the evolutionary struggle for survival, Mother Nature has already produced a variety of poisons and biological weapons that are far more sophisticated than anything humans have come up with—and they can appear at the most unexpected of times.

Trofim Lysenko and Soviet Science

During the reign of Joseph Stalin, Soviet science was dominated by Trofim Lysenko, who rejected modern science and replaced it with a mishmash of pseudoscience and ideology. His thirty-year reign led to the imprisonment or death of hundreds of scientists and illustrated the dangers of placing "science" under ideological control—but also demonstrated that, in the end, real science simply cannot be repressed.

When the Communist Party took over Russia in 1917, they turned all of orthodox Marxist ideology on its head. For decades, Socialist theorists had declared that human society evolved over time through laws of economic development as one "stage" of history replaced another—and the ideology of Marxism (or "scientific socialism", as it was also called) gave them the ability to use these economic laws to predict the future development of society. Modern capitalist society would inevitably, they declared, be replaced by a socialist society.

But when the socialist revolution happened in 1917, it was not in modern capitalist Europe or America—it was in Russia, a backwards undeveloped agricultural society where "capitalism" barely existed. By the time Joseph Stalin established himself as the sole dictator, Soviet theorists had already developed an ideology which "explained" why they had been able to seize power in an area where every Marxist orthodoxy said they could not have: the Stalinists declared that the entire idea of "natural laws of development" was wrong, and that ideology and pure political power could allow them to step outside of history and produce a "New Soviet Man", who could bend nature and history to his own will in any direction he desired. It was a framework into which Trofim Lysenko fitted perfectly.

Lysenko had been born into a poor rural peasant family in 1898. After the Russian Revolution he became an agronomist, studied plant science, and began working on an agricultural research station in Azerbaijan. During this time, the science of biology was exploding, as Darwinian evolutionary theory was combined with the Mendelian theory of genes and heredity to produce the

"Modern Synthesis", our current framework of DNA, mutations, selection and evolution. Lysenko, however, rejected this framework, and clung to the old "Lamarckian" hypothesis, which declared that characteristics aquired during life could be inherited by the offspring: a blacksmith who developed large muscular arms during his lifetime, for instance, would in turn have children who were born with large muscular arms. Applying this reasoning to agriculture, Lysenko opined that he could change the growing characteristics of plants by exposing their seeds and seedlings to differing environmental conditions, and that these changes would then be passed on through the seeds. In 1927, he carried out a series of experiments in which he placed peas in cold temperatures, then grew the plants—and found that the resulting pea plants not only tolerated cold growing conditions, but passed this trait on in their own seeds. He also found that by exposing wheat grains to cold and wet conditions before planting them, he could convert summer wheat into winter wheat. Lysenko called his process "vernalization", and he became something of a sensation when the Communist Party newspaper *Pravda* wrote stories on his "discoveries".

In reality, Lysenko's experiments were poorly designed, incompetently carried out, and based on flawed data from small sample sizes. But in Stalin's Soviet Union, what really mattered was political ideology, and Lysenko fit perfectly into Stalin's "Marxist-Leninist" political ideology. As the son of a poor peasant family, Lysenko was the perfect political symbol for the Soviet regime's celebration of "proletarian" culture over that of the "decadent bourgeoisie", and Lysenko was lauded as a "barefoot scientist", who illustrated the superiority of the workers in the "class struggle" and the benefits of "practical work" over sterile "bourgeois idealism". Lysenko's idea that the characteristics of plants could be altered at will also fit perfectly with Stalin's political ideology that his regime could produce the New Soviet Man and mold the perfect classless society. And finally, Lysenko's "discoveries" opened up a new method for dealing with one of the largest difficulties faced by the Soviet Government—the near-destruction of the Russian agricultural sector during the "collectivization" fights of the 1930's. Using Lysenko's "vernalization" techniques, Stalin hoped to rapidly expand Soviet agricultural output and end the famines and widespread rural discontent that his heavy-handed policies had caused.

With Stalin's personal approval, Lysenko's rise in the Soviet regime was rapid. He was given control of an agricultural institute in Odessa to continue his experiments, which he published in a new journal titled "Vernalization". (His published results were highly selective—trumpeting even the smallest "success" but neglecting to mention any of the numerous failures.) As the de facto ideological Pope of Soviet science, Lysenko also expanded upon his Lamarckian theories of biology, arguing that Mendel and Darwin were wrong, there were no such things as "genes", and that plants and animals developed solely according to the environment within which they were raised. Under Stalin's orders, huge portions of agricultural land on collective farms and state farms began to be planted according to Lysenko's "vernalization" methods.

This, of course, was simply pseudo-scientific nonsense—and Soviet biologists knew this and said so. The result was swift and draconian. Stalin ordered that all science education in the USSR be brought into ideological line with Lysenkoism, declared that Mendelian or Darwinian thought was reactionary "menshevist idealism", and that criticism of Lysenko or his ideas was tantamount to criticism of Marxism-Leninism and the Communist Party (and Stalin). Thousands of Soviet scientists were stripped of their positions and sent to work in factories. Hundreds were arrested and charged as "counter-revolutionaries" who were "sabotaging Soviet agriculture". Many of them were shot; many more died in gulags.

Yet through the thirty years of ideological and physical repression that accompanied Lysenko's reign, the simple fact remained that Lysenko's "science" was demonstrably wrong, and a small but brave contingent of Soviet scientists continued to say so. Most prominent of these was geneticist Nikolai Vavilov, who, upon his arrest and trial in 1939, bluntly told the court, "We shall go the pyre, we shall burn, but we shall not retreat from our convictions. I tell you, in all frankness, that I believed and still believe and insist on what I think is right.... This is a fact, and to retreat from it simply because some occupying high posts desire it is impossible." Vavilov died in prison in 1943.

When Stalin died in 1953, Lysenko lost the basis of his political and ideological power. Stalin's successor, Nikita Krushchev, was also the son of a poor peasant, and at first he continued to back Lysenko. But Krushchev made it a priority to "de-Stalinize" the Soviet Union (after all, Stalin's purges had wiped out most of the Communist Party ruling clique), and Lysenkoism had been an important prop to Stalin. So, when Krushchev made his "secret speech" to the Communist Party Congress denouncing Stalin and his "personality cult", and relaxed the censorship in the state press to allow criticism of Stalin and his methods, Lysenko also inevitably became a target. The remaining remnants of Soviet science, including prominent physicist Andrei Sakharov, denounced Lysenko and his crackpot theories. In 1964, Lysenko was officially removed from his post as head of the Institute of Genetics at the Academy of Sciences, and was sent to a small research farm in Moscow, where he fell into disgrace and forgotten obscurity before dying in 1975. He had indirectly killed and imprisoned thousands of Soviet researchers and set Russian biology back by decades, and his wrong-headed agricultural methods had led to famines that killed millions of people.

Today, the Lysenko affair is remembered as an object lesson in what happens when a society attempts to force science to base itself on favored political or social doctrine. Throughout history, every time that someone has attempted to impose an ideology onto science, whether it was the Catholic Church and Galileo, or Lysenko and the Soviet Union, or today's global-warming deniers and anti-vaccine pseudoscientists, it has ended in disaster.

But at the same time, the Lysenko affair gives us hope: it demonstrates that real science cannot be suppressed, even if it is opposed by a brutal ideological regime that literally kills its opponents. Science is the study of reality, and reality simply cannot be hidden. In the end, science always wins.

Malls: A History of the Suburban Shopping Mecca

The indoor shopping mall is an American icon. They can be found in nearly every suburban area in the US. But these temples of consumerism were first designed by a socialist, who wanted to create a common community. And today, the "mall" is quietly fading from the scene.

The "shopping mall" is an old concept. Ancient Rome had its Forum, which was lined with rows of open-air shops selling everything from pottery to wine and bread. And for 2,000 years afterwards, every sizable town or city had its central marketplace where merchants and artisans could gather to hawk their wares. As European and American society became more and more urbanized during the late 19th and early 20th century, this custom became codified into the "downtown", the inner-city "business district" where streets were lined with row upon row of shops and restaurants.

But by the 1940's, however, "downtowns" were declining as some of the harsher realities of urban life began to set in. Urban city centers were crowded, dirty, and unpleasant places. The new American "car culture" increased the congestion and pollution. Cobblestone streets that were once open avenues for pedestrians and bicyclists now became snarled with traffic and parking. "Downtowns" became areas of poverty and crime. And as more and more people fled to the suburbs to escape the city (in the civil-rights-era US, much of this was due to "white flight", as the well-off moved out of town to avoid having to deal with "those people"), they were left without any easy access to the downtown shopping areas.

Enter Victor Gruen. Gruen had been born in Austria, where, during his lifetime, he had seen the once-quaint city centers of Europe turn from pedestrian shops and cafes to smoke-belching urban quagmires. When the Nazis came to power in Germany and annexed Austria, Gruen, who was a Socialist and a Jew, was targeted for arrest, and he fled to the United States in 1938.

As an architect, Gruen also brought with him a vision—a conception of a new type of city which would do away with the crowded and dirty commercial streets of downtown (he called them "avenues of horror") and replace them with a modern version of the old traditional town square, where pedestrians once again strolled past shops, parks, fountains, outdoors cafes, and theaters. As a Socialist, Gruen wanted to bring people together, to gather in common places and form a community—so his "malls" would be surrounded by houses, office buildings and workplaces, all within walking distance. (Gruen hated "cars", with all their noise and congestion and pollution.) And, in the innovation that would change the commercial world, Gruen planned to enclose the entire "town square" within a set of walls and a roof, to protect all of the pedestrian shoppers from the weather (and also from any of their fellow citizens who might be criminally-inclined). In effect, Gruen planned to bring the best parts of the city "inside", and to keep the rest "outside".

Gruen first presented his concept in 1943, when the trade magazine *Architectural Forum* ran a contest for the "postwar city of the future". The editors were not impressed.

But in the 1950's, Gruen finally got his chance. For several years, suburban areas had been constructing their own small versions of "downtown", to give their residents a place to shop without having to go into the city. These consisted of two or three large department stores with rows of small open-air independent shops and restaurants in between. Gruen himself designed such a "strip mall", called Northland, outside of Detroit. Then in 1952, the Dayton's Department Store chain made plans to open a new shopping center in Edina MN, a suburb of Minneapolis. It was to be called "Southdale". They hired Victor Gruen to design it, and gave him a free hand. For the first time, he could bring his vision to life.

The Southdale Mall, as it came to be known, opened in 1956. It was an amazing new concept for the time. The Mall consisted of two large department stores, Dayton's and Donaldson's, with a row of 72 small shops, stacked in two floors, in between. But the pedestrian "avenue" was enclosed within a single building, almost as large as an entire city block. Glass roofs allowed sunlight to stream in. The central courtyard, overlooked by the upper level of shops, had fountains and potted trees and flower gardens. There was an aviary with caged songbirds, and a fish pond with waterfalls. Surrounding the courtyard were a number of restaurants and cafes, with tables set up for "outdoors dining", indoors. Here, Gruen hoped, people could gather to talk and stroll and debate and socialize just as people used to do in the old town squares and boulevards of Paris and Berlin and Vienna. And the entire massive structure was enclosed and heated—instead of slogging downtown through snow and slush, shoppers could sip coffee at the cafes comfortably in their shirtsleeves even as the harsh Minnesota winters raged outside. It was, as the Mall's advertising trumpeted, an "Eternal Spring". Nothing like it had ever been seen before. On the day the Southdale Mall opened, 75,000 people crowded in to experience it.

The effect was electric—literally. Every suburban area in the US and Canada suddenly wanted its own Mall. For most, the local Mall was the only place in town they could go that was heated in the winter and air-conditioned in the summer. They became favored hangouts for teens (who quickly became known as "mallrats"). During the next few decades, over a thousand indoor malls opened, with each one vying to be larger and grander than the last. When the West Edmonton Mall opened near Alberta, Canada in 1981, it was dubbed a "mega-mall": it had 800 shopping stores, a hotel, an indoors amusement and water park with rides, an artificial indoors lake, a zoo, and a church. Near Minneapolis MN, the birthplace of Gruen's "mall", the Mall of America opened in 1992; today it has 520 stores and is the largest mall in the US (it was the subject of its own TV series). But even the American mega-malls were eclipsed in the 2010's as newly-rich Asian nations like China constructed their own versions. The Golden Resources Mall in Beijing has over 1,000 stores, making it twice as big as the Mall of America.

Gruen, meanwhile, was horrified. He had planned his enclosed "town square" as part of a larger community, in which shopping, workspaces, homes and recreational areas would all be integrated into one pedestrian-based community, remaking and transforming the modern city. Instead, suburban malls turned into big sprawling money-making machines, drawing the cars that Gruen hated from the cities out to the suburbs and sucking consumers in for all-day shopping sprees. In 1968, Gruen left the United States and moved back to Austria, where he denounced the phenomenon that he had created, referring to shopping malls as his "bastard developments". He died in 1980.

And today, the malls he created are being killed as well. By the 1990's, the spiralling growth of suburban shopping malls had become unsustainable. New malls began cannibalizing old ones, luring away their customers and putting them out of business. Former mall staples such as Toys R Us or Barnes and Noble began leaving the malls and opening their own super-stores. The 2008 Great Recession hit malls hard, and no new large indoors mall has been built in the US since 2009. Consumer tastes also began to change—after spending all day inside at work, people now wanted to go outside to relax. City governments began to modernize and revitalize their "downtown" districts, turning them into "lifestyle centers" in which entertainment, shopping, and green areas occupy large open areas of space, alongside office buildings and apartments. Ironically, it is a concept that is much closer to Gruen's original vision.

How Teddy Roosevelt Won the Nobel Peace Prize

In 1906, Theodore Roosevelt was awarded the Nobel Peace Prize, for helping to negotiate an end to the Russo-Japanese War. Roosevelt was the first of four American Presidents to win the Prize.

At the end of the 19th century, eastern Asia was an arena of conflict. The prize was China. The vast country, with its numerous resources and its huge potential commercial market, was far too weak to defend itself from outsiders, and was occupied by a number of Western powers. Germany had control of several Chinese ports; the British held large coastal areas and had fought the Opium Wars to protect its commercial interests. The United States, which had just entered the world stage after beating Spain in the Spanish-American War in 1898, had declared its "Open Door" policy in China (guaranteeing free American access to the Chinese market) to expand its own commercial and military interests in the Pacific.

Another newcomer was Japan. For centuries Japan had closed itself off from the world, expelling foreigners and closing its ports to outsiders. But after the United States sent a naval fleet to Tokyo force a treaty, the Japanese realized that their only survival strategy was to beat the West at their own game and to become an imperial power herself. After the Meiji Restoration in 1868, Japan under its new Emperor began an enthusiastic program of "modernization". Western styles of dress were adopted, and students were sent to universities all over the world to be trained in Western science, economics and technology. The traditional *samurai* warrior class was abolished, and a modern Army and Navy, trained by British and German officers, was formed. By 1894, Japan was strong enough to claim her own piece of China, seizing Korea and Taiwan in the Sino-Japanese War. And when Japanese ambitions then turned towards Manchuria, it brought her into direct conflict with Russia.

By the first decade of the 20th century, the Russian Empire, ruled by Tsar Nicholas II, was already rotting from the inside. It was a backward agrarian nation that lacked modern industry, and it was torn by political rebellion against its autocratic government. But Russia had a huge Army and Navy, and was still considered a world-class military power. Most of the territory that Japan now coveted in the Far East was claimed by the Tsar, and Russia had a large naval base at Port Arthur to protect it. If the Japanese wanted to sieze their own piece of Asia, they would have to deal with the Russians.

In February 1904, the Japanese made their move, with a surprise attack on Port Arthur. Thousands of Japanese troops swarmed ashore and, although they failed to capture the fortress, they did surround it and kept it cut off from the rest of the war, as other Japanese troops siezed coastal areas in Manchuria. The Tsar dispatched his Baltic Fleet to the area; both he and the rest of Europe, confident in the superiority of the "white race" over the "Asiatics", assumed he would quickly crush the Japanese upstarts. Instead, to everyone's shock, the Imperial Japanese Navy intercepted the Russian Fleet in the Straits of Tsushima in May 1905, and completely destroyed it.

But now the Japanese faced a problem. Although they had proven themselves militarily superior to the Russians, Japan did not have the enormous manpower reserves or economy that Russia did, and did not have the necessary resources to carry the war through to the end. So the Japanese Emperor looked for a diplomatic solution through a negotiated peace, and turned to the United States for help, asking President Theodore Roosevelt if he would act as a mediator with the Russians.

Roosevelt had his own expansionist reasons for becoming involved. The US had territories in the Pacific, including Hawaii, the Philippines, and Guam, and also had its own commercial interests in China. The Japanese, with their willingness to use military force in the cause of expansionism, had demonstrated that they were now potential rivals, and Roosevelt wanted to limit their territorial expansion as much as possible. So when the US agreed to the Japanese diplomatic request, it had its own agenda in mind. Roosevelt agreed to act as an intermediary only after Japan first agreed to accept the US "Open Door" policy in China.

At first, Russia flatly refused negotiations. Despite his heavy military losses, the Tsar was still convinced that he would win. It took an extraordinarily blunt diplomatic message from US Ambassador George Meyer, informing the Russian Government that not only the US but all of Europe believed that the Russians would be defeated by Japan and lose all of their Asian possessions, to change the Tsar's mind. He reluctantly agreed to send a representative to negotiations to be held in Portsmouth Navy Yard.

When the talks began in August 1905, the two sides were far apart. Japan wanted all the territory it had conquered during the war to be permanently ceded to it, and also wanted Russia to pay a lump sum of money as "war reparations". Russia refused both demands. Roosevelt went into action behind the scenes, talking with representatives from both sides and encouraging them to find common ground for a settlement. Through diplomatic channels, he talked other world leaders into pressuring Tsar Nicholas for concessions (including Nicholas's cousins, King George of England and Kaiser

Wilhelm of Germany), and also sent cables to the Japanese Government advising it to not be "greedy" and to moderate its territorial demands.

In September 1905, agreement was finally reached. Japan would be allowed to keep a portion of the territory she occupied, and Russia would not be obligated to make any payments of reparations or indemnities. The Treaty of Portsmouth ended the Russo-Japanese War.

In 1906, in recognition of his diplomatic success in ending the war, Teddy Roosevelt became the first American to win a Nobel Peace Prize. The award was not without controversy. Many European leftists considered Roosevelt to be an unapologetic imperialist who had seized territory for the Panama Canal and had waged a bloody counter-insurgency in the Philippines, and whose actions therefore made him unsuitable for a Peace Prize. There were also whispers that the Nobel Committee itself had political reasons for awarding Roosevelt: when the Nobel Prize Committee had been formed, Norway was a part of Sweden, but in 1906 Norway had just become an independent nation, and it was suspected by many that the Norwegian committee that awarded the Peace Prize was trying to kiss up to America in a bid to win political support for Norway from an emerging world power. Roosevelt himself would go on to advocate the creation of an international political organization that would have "police power"—but then he opposed American affiliation with the League of Nations in 1919.

The issues that sparked the Russo-Japanese War, meanwhile, were never settled. Japan was still determined to carve out an empire of her own in East Asia, and after fighting on the side of the Entente Allies in the First World War, Japan would invade Manchuria in the 1930's, leading to direct conflict with the United States in the Second World War.

Billy Joel and "Allentown"

In 1982, recording artist Billy Joel released a single titled "Allentown". The song painted a picture of a depressed American economy and the decline of the US as a world economic power, through the eyes of a single city crippled by the disappearance of its manufacturing industries.

At the end of the Second World War, much of the world lay in ruins. The major cities in Europe and Asia had been bombed into ruins, industrial capacity had been destroyed, and the economy was shattered. Years of reconstruction lay ahead.

But one major power had escaped the destruction. No enemy bombers had reached the United States; its factories and industries were intact. In the 1950's and 1960's, the US became an economic superpower, as rising wages, increasing purchasing power, and continuously-expanding industrial output turned America into the most powerful economy in human history. US products and consumer culture dominated the entire world.

That began to change in the 1970's, as Europe and Asia began to recover from the devastation of World War II. Former enemies in Germany and Japan (now allies) finally reached and then exceeded their pre-war economic levels. In one industry after another, including steel, electronics, automobiles, and chemicals, Japanese and German companies first pushed American companies out of their dominating global market share, and then invaded the US itself, capturing an ever-larger share of the American consumer economy.

The effect in the US was crushing. As the American economy became mired in "stagflation", major companies like Bethlehem Steel, Zenith, and General Motors began losing ground to newer, more modernized and more efficient companies like Nippon Steel, BMW, Toyota, and Panasonic. In a desperate attempt to stay in the game, American companies began extracting "give-backs" from their worker unions, forcing deep cuts in wages and benefits in exchange for promises to not close the plants (promises that were usually un-kept).

"Runaway factories" left the US in droves for low-wage havens in Mexico, then in China. In the US, once-powerful labor unions disappeared as plants closed and workers were laid off, and unemployment rose to levels not seen since the 30's. Economists began to talk about a permanent "post-industrial economy", in which low-wage non-union "service-sector" jobs would be the new norm. Throughout the Northeast, the collection of now-closed and empty factories that dotted the landscape became known as "The Rust Belt".

Singer-songwriter Billy Joel had already reached the top of the charts with his hit album "The Stranger". For his latest album, "The Nylon Curtain", he wanted to do a song about the decline of American manufacturing and the economic ruin it was leaving behind. At first, he centered the song around Levittown, the company-owned industrial city in New York that Joel had grown up near. "Well we're living here in Levittown, and I don't see much going down", the lyrics began. But although he worked out a musical chord progression that he liked, Joel couldn't make the lyrics fall into place. At heart, Billy Joel was a story-teller, and he couldn't see a good interesting story here, and thought his lyrics would be "boring". He set the song aside.

Then a few years later in 1981, while preparing to record "The Nylon Curtain", he took a trip to the Lehigh Valley, Pennsylvania, and became interested in the history of the steel industry and the problems it was currently facing. That gave him the story he wanted to tell. Although the steel industry was centered in Bethlehem, Joel thought that "Allentown" sounded better in the lyrics and was easier to rhyme. (He also concluded that people would think that a song about "Bethlehem" was a Christmas song.) And so the lyrics for "Levittown" became re-worked into "Allentown". As he explained later, "It sounds like Jimmytown, Bobbyburgh, Anytown. It just sounds real American."

The song, over an acoustic background of steam whistles, factory machinery and industrial hammers, paints a picture of a place where the factories are shut down and the former workers are standing in lines and filling out forms at the unemployment office. Their fathers had fought World War Two and then built the most prosperous economy in the world, and their sons had assumed that their jobs at the steel mills would give them at least that same standard of living. Instead, their factories had closed, their jobs were gone, and they were left with nothing. "Allentown", Joel noted, "is a metaphor for America."

When the album and single were released in 1982, the Mayor of Allentown PA was Joe Dadonna, a colorful local character who had the difficult job of promoting the image of his city during the worst economic crisis of its history. While many locals viewed "Allentown" as a put-down of their declining city, Mayor Dadonna saw it as an opportunity for some publicity and promotion. He wrote a letter to Joel (and helpfully provided copies to the press) inviting him to do a concert in Allentown, and asking him to donate a portion of his royalties towards a scholarship for music students in the city.

Joel politely declined to set up a scholarship fund, explaining that he only worked with charities in his hometown of Levittown, but he did add Allentown to his tour schedule. In a fitting irony, the 1983 concert had to be held in nearby Bethlehem, because Allentown had no show arena. Joel closed the show with "Allentown", was given a standing ovation, and was then presented with honorary residence and a key to the city by Dadonna, who told him he had written "a gritty song about a gritty city". Joel modestly replied "I just wrote a song, I'm not Thomas Edison. Let's not blow it all out of proportion."

America's Jack the Ripper: The Austin Serial Killer

In 1884, the city of Austin TX was gripped by what newspapers called "an epidemic of murder". Seven women and one man were killed in horrific fashion by what was dubbed "The Servant Girl Annihilator". It was one of America's first serial killers.

The years after the Civil War were painful ones for the United States, especially in the former Confederacy. The postwar Reconstruction had forced social and racial changes onto an unwilling Southern culture, and tensions were high. The Ku Klux Klan, formed by former Confederate soldiers, was carrying out terrorist attacks on African-American former slaves, and would soon grow to national prominence. The traditional plantation economy was slowly being replaced by urbanization.

By 1884, the city of Austin TX had become a symbol of the new South. Called by some "The Athens of the West", the city had over 25,000 inhabitants and three colleges, including the University of Texas. Electric lights had begun to appear in the city's streets, and telephones linked residents together.

When the first murder happened, it attracted little attention. A young African-American woman named Mollie Smith worked as a cook for a prominent white family, and lived in a small apartment attached to the house with her boyfriend Walter Spencer. On the night of December 29, 1884, someone broke into the apartment, knocked Spencer unconscious with an axe blow to the head, and dragged Mollie outside. Her body was found next to the outhouse: she had been raped, and her skull split with an axe.

Then, in May 1885, the body of Eliza Shelly was found after screams were heard coming from her servant's cabin. Shelly, an African-American, worked as a live-in cook for a former Texas state legislator. She had also been killed with an axe.

The murders continued. In late May, Irene Cross was stabbed, sliced open, and scalped. Found barely alive, she lived just long enough to give a decription of her killer: a heavy-set African-American man. A few months later, eleven-year-old Mary Ramey was raped and stabbed through the ear with a thin iron bar. She bled to death shortly after being found. On September 28, Gracie Vance and her boyfriend Orange Washington were both killed with an axe, and two friends staying with them were wounded.

All of these victims were African-Americans who worked as cooks or maids for wealthy white families, and were attacked at night in their servant's quarters. In most cases the murder weapon, a bloody axe, had been left behind at the scene.

Although "serial killers" are a depressingly familiar phenomenon in today's America, in 1885 this was something new, and the press, dubbing the unknown killer "The Servant Girl Annihilator", didn't know what to make of it. (The world-famous "Jack the Ripper" serial killings in London were still several years away.) The Austin police were headed by Chief Grooms Lee, the son of a local politician who was bedeviled by rumors of embezzlement; several of the city's twelve police officers were themselves suspected of carrying out robberies. Since the Annihilator seemed to be targeting only African-Americans, the crimes were a low priority for the police.

That changed on Christmas Eve 1885. A white woman named Susan Hancock was found dead by her husband. Her head had been split by an axe, and her body left in the backyard. An hour later, another body was discovered: another white woman, Eula Phillips, was found dead, and her husband James had been struck in the head with an axe and left for dead.

With the "Christmas Eve Massacre", the city went into a panic. Proposals were made to post soldiers on the streets at night as sentries. The police force was increased to fifty. Police Chief Lee began having his officers randomly stop young black men and question them—and on at least one occasion the police beat a suspect and threatened to lynch him if he didn't confess. The press was told that bloody bare footprints had been found at several of the crime scenes, indicating that the killer had removed his shoes to prevent making any noise as he approached his victims. One significant detail, however, had been withheld from the press—one of the footprints indicated that the Servant Girl Annihilator had only four toes on his right foot.

The police, however, decided that the murders of the two white women were not the work of the Annihilator, despite the similarities. Instead, they concluded that both women had been killed by their own husbands, in a drunken or jealous rage—perhaps using an axe to throw suspicion away from themselves. In separate trials, James Philips was convicted of the murder of his wife Eula (the conviction was later overturned on appeal), and Moses Hancock was acquitted of the murder of his wife Susan.

In February 1886, a 20-year-old African-American man named Nathan Elgin, in a drunken rage, dragged a young black woman out of an Austin saloon and into the street, where he began beating her. A policeman quickly arrived, and when Elgin turned on him with a knife, he shot Elgin and killed him. At the autopsy, it turned out that Elgin had only four toes on his right foot. There were no further Annihilator murders after Elgin's death. Today, most researchers conclude that Elgin was likely responsible for all of the crimes.

20099537R00115

Printed in Great Britain
by Amazon